THE
KAMTA
PRIMER

A Practical Shamanic Guide for using Kemetic Ritual, Magick and Spirituality for Acquiring Power

Derric Moore

Published by:	Four Sons Publications
Contact:	1 SōL Alliance Co. P.O. Box 596 Liberal, KS 67905-0596 www.1solalliance.com

Copyright © 2017 Derric Moore

All rights reserved. No part of this publication may be reproduced or transmitted in any form or by any means, electronic or mechanical, including photocopying, recording or by any information storage and retrieval system, without written permission from the author, except for the inclusion of brief quotation in a review.

Portion of this book were previously published in *MAA AANKH: Finding God the Afro-American Way by Honoring the Ancestors and Guardian Spirits*, and Seven Steps to Understanding God by Derric Moore, Four Sons Publication, in Copyright 2010, and Kamta: A Practical Kemetic Path for Obtaining Power by Derric Moore, Four Sons Publication, in Copyright 2011,

The information contained in this book is intended to be educational and not for diagnosis, prescription, or treatment of any health disorder whatsoever. This information should not replace consultation with a competent healthcare professional. The content of the book is intended to be used as an adjunct to a rational and responsible healthcare program prescribed by a licensed healthcare practitioner. This is a book about faith. As such the author and publisher do not warrant the success any person would have using any of the exercises and techniques contained herein. Success and failure will vary. The author and publisher therefore are in no way liable for any misuse of the material contained herein.

To protect the identity and privacy of others, most of the names within this book have been adapted, modified and changed for confidentiality purposes. Any resemblance to real persons, living or dead is purely coincidental.

Includes Index
Cover art and Illustrations by: Derric "Rau Khu" Moore
Ramses and Watsui Rwanda photo public domain
Photos courtesy of Dreamstine.com

ISBN: 978-0985506759

Publication Date: September 6, 2017

Printed in the United States of America

CONTENTS

INTRODUCTION V

PART ONE: THE TOOLS OF KAMTA 1
  ONE: WHAT IS KAMTA? 3
    Lesson One: Preparing for Spiritual Exchange 32
  TWO: FINDING YOUR MAA AANKH 45
    Lesson Two: Primary Steps for
    Conducting Rituals 61
  THREE: ACKNOWLEDGING THE CALL 65
    Lesson Three: Working with the Honorable Dead 99
  FOUR: THE GUARDIAN SPIRITS 117
    Lesson Four: Basic Instructions on
    Working with the Netcharu (Guardian Spirits) 137

PART TWO: PRACTICING KAMTA 147
  FIVE: WHY WERE WE CREATED 149
    Lesson Five: Discovering Your Purpose 161
  SIX: BECOMING MAA KHRU (BORN AGAIN
  KEMETICALLY) 165
    Lesson Six: Recognizing Your Set 181
  SEVEN: CREATING A MAGICKAL WAY OF LIFE 187
    Lesson Seven: Regular Rituals 200

PARTING WORDS 205
APPENDIX 206
SELECT BIBLIOGRAPHY 214
INDEX 217

ACKNOWLEDGMENTS

THANK YOU Nebertchar, our Perfect Creator and Lord of All for this wonderful experience and opportunity to experience life. Thank you for every success and every obstacle put in my way to make me better.

Thank you aakhu for all the sacrifices that were made for me to enjoy the freedoms and liberties I have today.

Thank you netcharu., great guardian spirits of us all who protect the mysteries of the Divine.

Thanks to my loving wife, my family and friends, for your love, support and agreeing to disagree until further notice.

Special thanks as always to Ms. B, Papa Raul, Ms. Smith, and Iya, whose teachings I am still reflecting upon to this day.

Thank you all you teachers whose paths I have crossed, who have helped me in one way or another.

INTRODUCTION

It began as a typical mathematics exam. I taught a math class over the summer, so I was sitting in class reading a book, while watching my students go through the usual self-talk as they took their math exam. Their expressions remind me of how once upon a time, I was each of these students. As I look at each student, I think:

"They are probably going to get an A on this test," I gleefully said to myself with a smirk as I observed the confidence and poise a few of the students who mastered the concepts and were completing the problems with relative ease.

"They will probably do good," I thought of the other students who came in during the week prior to the exam to get a better understanding of the concept. They have not mastered the concepts but they practiced and are almost there. I could see them questioning themselves in their face. They are fighting with themselves. They still struggled with certain concepts but they will work through the problem. I am proud of them because they have come a long way.

Then, I say to myself about the few remaining students. "God, I hope they pass." I know these students needed help in understanding concepts but they refused to come in. They had a million + 1 excuse as to why they could not and would not get any help. They refused to practice the concepts. I told these few students over and over again, that mathematics is a language and just like you cannot memorize a language, you cannot memorize mathematics. The problems are always changing but the concepts are always the same. Now they are trying to take an exam that they are in no shape, fashion or form prepared for. "I wish they had come in."

Trying not to get too depressed by the inevitable that I am going to have to grade an exam of a student that is most likely going to fail. I return to reading my book.

Next, as the time winds down, I prepare to ask each one of them how they think they did, to determine if I explained the concept to them clearly and. Then I tell them to have a good weekend as they exit the classroom.

It is always the same. The students who mastered the concept and are confident they are going to get an 'A', usually are the first to finish. All except one or two of them—who have learned from their past mistakes of taking exams, so they are triple and quadruple checking their work in order to get as close to a 100 percent as possible. Anyway, most of these students humbly say the exam was okay but I can always see their enthusiasm in their facial expressions. They are usually ready to explode and they can't wait to get outside of the classroom to compare thoughts on the exam and predict the grade they will receive with their peers.

The students who worked and struggled exit next. They are usually not as confident but hopeful. They usually tell me that they "think" they did alright, which usually means they tried real hard based upon what they remember. Most of these students crammed the night before, so I know. I am grading their memory, not their understanding of the material. I will have to reteach them until the lightbulb finally comes on.

The remaining students in the class are the ones that did not come in get help. These students can be divided into two groups:

Group #1) the ones who do not care and, Group #2) the excuse makers. Group #1 basically do not care. These students lack the maturity to be in the class, so they do not take it seriously. These students usually will drop out of school and return after they had to work in the real world and start a family. That's when they will get serious and when asked how they think they did. They usually hunch their shoulders and joke about how they failed. Group #2, the excuse makers do not want to fail the exam but they are not serious about passing it either. Many times, they expect to learn everything just by simply listening to a lecture but when asked to get help on their math work. That is when they give all of these excuses: e.g. they did not have time, their job, etc. I have heard it all before and what it sounds like to me is they do not know how to manage their time. Again, something I can help them with if they take the time to come see me. Along with the 'A' student, Group #2 are usually the last to finish the exam.

I had seen it before. It is the same thing every test but this examination was different. As the students filed out after completing the examination. There was a lady from Group #2 who was trying to complete her exam. Seeing that no one was around except me, she let out an outburst that shattered the silence,

"Oh God...help me!"

The outburst was so loud and unexpected, that it startled me and took me back to one day when I was taking an exam and cried out the same thing. I felt sorry for her because she had done everything, she knew she could physically do. But her prayers were still going to go unanswered because she did not have the real knowledge of how to move God.

You see, all religious and spiritual traditions have what is called exoteric and esoteric knowledge. Exoteric knowledge is basically the outward display of a religion or tradition (e.g. written texts, attire, etc.) that would-be-followers and adherents can grasp using their mind and intellect, in order to make sense of their daily lives. Because of there is so much information, the exoteric knowledge usually requires a hierarchy to ensure that the fundamental beliefs and practices of the religion or tradition are properly distributed. Over time, exoteric knowledge that follows this fundamental path becomes a dogma and in extreme cases fundamentalism.

Esoteric knowledge is more closely related to the mysteries of the universe and the mind. It is based upon understanding who and what our Creator is and what is our relationship to It. Unlike exoteric knowledge, esoteric knowledge was not usually found in volumes of books because in ancient times it was only shared with a selected clandestine few. Since there was not a large amount of exoteric information that was written, esoteric knowledge usually did not require a hierarchy because most of the individuals who are on this path are usually classified as being strange and crazy because they think outside of the box, and do not conform to the norm. However, as time passes, these individuals are honored and respected as being visionaries, mystics, prophets and shamans.

In order for religions and spiritual traditions to prosper and grow, both exoteric and esoteric knowledge must be shared in order to keep the practice fresh, or they become like stagnant water. What this lady was experiencing was a breakdown of her old ways, which were not working because the esoteric knowledge had not been shared with her. In other words, this lady was failing because she was taught to beg God (and everyone else if possible) to save her, instead of being taught to tap into the power of God to save herself. This lady suffered from a classic case of lack of knowledge of self because she was not educated about the mysteries of her soul.

Many of us suffer from this same spiritual ailment in other areas of our life. There are brilliant minds chained to dead end jobs, communities in shambles due to unfocused political dreams, and countless good people who are incarcerated because this spiritual ailment prevents them from them all from creating their own solutions.

If the esoteric knowledge was shared with this lady, rather than praying to God outside of her. She would have prayed or done a ritual to move and stir the emotions within her being because her problems were not in her belief in God. Her problem was that she lacked self-control and discipline to achieve her goal. It was these forces within her that were preventing her from taking responsibility of her education and succeeding. I remembered I had a similar problem one time when taking a math exam and even more serious issues that led me to cry out to God. But after years of research and experimentation, I learned how to get my prayers answered through shamanism.

Although the term shaman has been used by scientists, historians and laymen alike as a general term to classify and describe traditional healers, seers, diviners, etc. from all over the world. According Miranda Aldhouse-Green author of *The Quest for the Shaman*, a shaman "is a Siberian Tungus word and simply means 'ecstatic one.'"

Aldhouse-Green also states that shamanism "is not even a religion as such but rather a worldview system or a grammar of the mind." In a 1996 interview in the journal *Alternative Therapies*, "Shamanic Healing: We Are Not Alone, "(reproduced in the online journal Shamanism), Harner says that "the practice of shamanism is a method, not a religion. It coexists with established religions in many cultures" (Horrigan and Harner, "Shamanic Healing" par. 4). In other words, shamanism is a pre-dogma, pre-religious spiritual tradition that focus on achieving tangible results. Shamanism is believed to be the oldest practicing spiritual tradition in the world, next to ancestor veneration, because according to shamanistic beliefs. In order for us to live a secure and fulfilling life, shamanism stress that it is imperative that we use our spiritual capabilities to favorably influence our lives. It accomplishes this by providing the esoteric knowledge needed to tap into the undying Power of the Divine. The shamanic path written about within these pages is called Kamta.

Kamta is a spiritual tradition that is based upon the shamanic principles of Kemet (Ancient Egypt) and combined with the remnants of the Bantu-Kongo philosophy that survived slavery in North America. Kamta is not the recreation, resurrection, reconstruction or revitalization of the Kemetic religion of old. Kamta is a spiritual practice born out of necessity. That focuses on tapping into the Divine Power to improve one's life through divination, veneration of the aakhu (ancestors and spirit guides), and by working with the netcharu (guardian spirits). The uniqueness of Kamta is that 1) you do not have to join a group to implement its principles, and. 2) It can be practiced anywhere, at any time even at work, while at school or playing because the basis of the practice takes place within the mind and body alone.

The purpose of this book is to provide you with a practical how-to primer to Kemetic Shamanism, that is Kemetic/Kemetic spirituality IN THE RAW with little to no dogma. Although the information within this book is fully supported by historical research, what you are about to read is based upon my personal experience and will not coincide with traditional schools of thought. That being said, welcome to Kamta.

Derric "Rau Khu" Moore 20017

How to Use This Book?

Like most shamanic traditions, Kamta focuses on healing yourself through healing others because when you focus on improving the lives of others you inadvertently also improve your own. This is part of the Maa philosophy, so to get the best out of this book.

THIS BOOK HAS BEEN ORGANIZED as a practical step-by-step guide to learning and practicing Kemetic shamanism and practicing Kemetic magick. It has been written for beginners new to ancient African philosophy and more advanced practitioners who are interested in making practical use of their metaphysical knowledge.

Every ritual practice written within these pages have been successfully performed myself, so I can attest to their efficacy. However, since I do not know your level of awareness, it is strongly advised that the most important thing that you. Is not to believe anything you read within pages. Instead, I strongly encourage you to first read and reread if possible, the entire book if possible, before attempting any of the lessons. Test it and see if it resonates with you. If it does not, move on, no harm done.

To help you to understand these concepts and have fun while doing so, this book has divided into two parts:

"PART ONE: The Tools of KAMTA, "provides you with the basic tools needed to practice Kamta. You will learn how to pray, meditate, conduct rituals, build ancestral shrines, build spirit houses, and communicate with your ancestors and guardian spirits for higher purposes.

"**PART TWO: Practicing KAMTA,** "I think is the most important part of this book because if you do not practice spirituality. Then your magick will not always work because you only use it for emergencies, instead of making it a daily part of your life. The way to improve any talent or skill is through constant practice.

Unfortunately, because we live in a western society that separates spirituality from religion, religion from science, science from magick, and so on. Spirituality, religion, magick, etc. are all treated as if they are something that exists outside of nature. Consequently, the only time people pray, meditate, decide to do a ritual, etc. is when there is a serious problem and it is the last resort. Then, when it fails, they say that prayer, meditation, ritual, etc. is a sham. When in truth, they should've been praying, meditating, doing, rituals, etc. all along from the start. If they had taken this approach from the beginning, they may have arrived at a different outcome.

This is not how our ancient or even most recent beloved ancestors lived their lives. They included the spiritual element in every aspect of their mundane life because they understand that both the physical and spiritual realities were intertwined and interdependent upon one another. So, Part Two shows you how to use the tools from Part One for practical purposes by applying it with the philosophy.

PART ONE: The Tools of KAMTA

A physicist had a horseshoe hanging on the door of his laboratory. His colleagues were surprised and asked whether he believed that it would bring luck to his experiments. He answered, "No, I don't believe in superstitions. But I have been told that its woks even if you don't believe in it."

– R. L. Weber, *A Random Walk in Science*

ONE:
What is Kamta?

When I got married, my wife and I wanted to have a child. So, one day, out of nowhere my wife found one of my mythology books and she started reading about the Kemetic dwarf a het  netchar (guardian spirit of the home) Bes, who assists Nebhet, the netchart (feminine for netchar) of love, romance, money and conception. Now, I knew who Bes was or rather I knew what the archeologists and egyptologists (intentionally lowercased) said Bes was, which is why I purchased a small statue of him years ago. But I could not make a connection with Bes. I had painted his statue and created a het (spiritual house/altar) for him and everything, but nothing happened. Zilch. I could not make a connection, so I dismantled his het and put his statue up.

But, when my wife and I got married, she found one of my mythology books and the Bes statue. For some reason, she was inspired to put it in the living room. It was odd that she all of a sudden took an interest in Bes, as if he called her. In fact, I remember when I asked her why she was reading about Bes, she simply stated that "He's kinda' funny looking but cool."

Shortly after we begin placing little pieces of candy at his feet once a week. Then, a month later, I got a call from my wife while at a conference that she was pregnant.

Now, nothing strange or out of the ordinary occurred after that but occasionally I noticed that when my wife began complaining about back pains due to the pregnancy. I would break out into a dance, which made her laugh hysterically and then she would cheer up. When I finish dancing, I looked and saw Bes staring right at me. I realized that it was Bes who was dancing through me. As I looked and saw my wife rubbing her swollen belly, I realized that Tawaret, Bes' consort was not too far behind.

Then, one day we had a scare. My wife began spotting and was not able to see her physician. As you can imagine, she was scared, anxious, depressed and worried because she felt like her hands were tied and all we could do was wait. Now, that I had a connection with Bes I offered him a glass of beer and some more candy, that he protects this child and watch over my wife during this pregnancy.

Finally, when we went to see the doctor, we were told that everything was alright and the baby was developing as normal, while we listened to the baby's heartbeat. To this day, we continue to honor Bes for his assistance. The reason this little ritual worked is because it was magick. That's right magick!

You see, contrary to popular belief, magick is a powerful, wonderful, noble and very spiritual art that teaches you about yourself and reality, but magick also is a great way of improving your health, increasing your finances, finding love and increasing your luck. This is because magick is all about making your intentions real.

Every time you want to do something, you are expressing your intentions but your capability of achieving depends upon your mind and physical means. For instance, if you want a glass of water, you simply will your physical body to get a glass and pour some water. However, what about if you want to break a habit or increase your finances, improve your chances of finding true love, etc., then what do you do? Well, it is the same thing, but this time you simply put your intention out 'there' and let the Universe manifest what you want.

It is simple and the truth is that magick is natural and everyone uses magick to some degree. For instance, if you ever put on certain attire (a suit or dress) to go to a job interview. You were using a form of magick to influence the interviewers, so that they believe you are good worker who deserves the job. I know it doesn't seem like magick because you were not burning any candles and chanting some arcane words, but it was. What you were doing was magick. Here's another example, if you ever went on a romantic date and burned some candles, incense, etc. to set the mood, guess what? You were doing magick. The intention was that you were creating a certain mood in order to have a romantic evening. This is all magick, which about having a tiny leap of faith that your mind, emotions and will can influence the universe.

Magick works so long as you believe it does and unbeknownst to most. You do not need to believe in a particular god, angel or spirit. You also don't need to use a whole lot of visual aids and other tools like candles, oils, etc. In fact, true theologians know that magick works regardless of what you believe in because if it didn't. There would not be hundreds of religions with millions of adherents praying or doing magick to a specific deity getting magick or miracles done.

But, the reason you many of us think that we are not doing magick is because some of these religious institutions don't like to use the term magick and prefer to say 'prayer.' So instead of doing magick, they tell you to pray for the desired change you want. While other religious groups tell their adherents that magick is evil in order to convince them to follow their dogma. But as you can see, there is nothing evil about magick because as I have said, we all do it to some varying degree. The reason various religious groups have suppressed magick is because by convincing people to follow their dogma, they have total social control over their adherents' mind.

Thankfully, before religion was organized there was shamanism, which was the spiritual tradition that helped all people to develop spiritually. This book is about a form of shamanism that I call Kamta.

Kamta is a Kemetic shamanic spiritual tradition that draws heavily on Kemetic spirituality and the remnants of the Bantu-Kongo philosophy (African cosmology) that survived slavery in North America. Kamta is not the recreation, reconstruction or resurrection of the Kemetic religion because the Kemetic religion was created for an ancient African agrarian who lived in the desert alongside the Nile River and was governed by a king and queen. In other words, the Kemetic religion is not relevant our situation. However, the concepts and principles of the Kemetic religion, which can be found in all indigenous African derived spiritual systems are. By using the concepts and principles and combining them with the surviving Bantu-Kongo philosophy, we have Kamta, a spiritual system that allows anyone to tap into the spiritual realm for assistance.

Metaphysically speaking, we say KAMTA (all caps) when referring to "the Black Lands" as an Afrocentric reference to the ancestors of the Kemetic people, the Kushites (Ancient Nubians), the ancestors of the African American South, and the spiritual world, which is imagined to be dark, hidden and invisible. KAMTA is the Dark Side but it has nothing to do with morals. It is a metaphorical allusion to the richness of the spiritual realm or kingdom of Osar, and the deepest parts of our mind.

Maa (Divine Balance) and Kemetic Thinking

Most of the confusion about the Kemetic people and their entire way of life is due to the fact that our Nilotic ancestors' texts, art, culture, history, philosophy, etc. has been interpreted by scholars (Westerners) who are from a culture that is totally alien to the Kemetic way of life. As A. A. Barb has stated in *The Legacy of Egypt* that "although scholars have since provided dictionaries and grammars of the ancient Egyptian language… [it] is not enough to grasp the Egyptian way of thinking, [that is] so utterly different from our Western logical mind."

To really understand the Kemetic culture, it must be understood that the Kemetic people were first and foremost Africans who lived, farmed and hunted in the East of Africa along the Nile River. This needs to be understood before we can even mention anything about the ethnicity and race of the people. Unfortunately, when Westerners try to understand and explain the Kemetic culture, they interpret it from a European and Arabic reference point or from a conqueror's perspective. It is like listening to a bully say they do not victimize others.

The fact is that Westerners and Arabs have never truly understood the Kemetic culture because it was foreign to them. Westerners and Arabs have always had difficulties in understanding the Kemetic (and all indigenous African cultures) because the Kemetic people were part pantheist, meaning they did not distinguish between the secular and the divine, but instead saw God in all things. They were also monistic believing that all of reality is composed of, and reducible to, a single substance.

To put it bluntly. Westerners have a long history of always interpreting any culture and religious belief outside of their own as inferior and primitive. There is no way a Jewish, Christian or Muslim scholar knowing the hell and havoc that has been created through their one-god, monotheistic beliefs can give an objective and unbiased interpretation of any indigenous religion. This is the reason the Afrocentric perspective is needed.

The basis of the Kemetic thought stems from their careful observation of nature, combined with their strong mystical intuition, which gave them profound insight into the sciences of life. Thus, the Kemetic people saw what we call the "real world" or the "world of mankind" as an artificial world with social etiquette and moral standards. To the Kemetic people, the "real world", the "true world" or the Maa (Divine Truth) could only be grasped by understanding nature. In this way, the Kemetic people could develop both a scientific attitude towards nature but also a deep mistrust for analytical thinking, which prevented them from being imbalanced in their thinking.

From the Kemetic perspective, life is not black and white but is always changing, which means there is no Absolute Good versus Absolute Evil, as in the Western and Arabic worldview. This is because what is good for one may not be necessary good for another. From the Kemetic perspective, too much and too little of anything is considered evil like, an excessive amount of sun and limited amount of water produces a desert. Or, an excessive amount of water and limited amount of sun results in flooding, hurricanes, etc. So, while Westerners and Arabs emphasize the duality between good and evil, while encouraging people to embrace good over evil. In Kemetic thinking these moral qualities are two extremes of a single scale where virtue does not rest in choosing one end or the other of this scale. Virtue is obtained by carefully maintaining a balance between these two extremes.

This concept is expressed in Kemetic thinking as Shu and Tefnut. Shu is associated with fullness, light, masculinity, action and heat, while Tefnut is associated with emptiness, darkness, femininity, passivity and coolness. The Kemetic people understood these traits at first glance appeared to be oppositional but this was an illusion because these two states required one another. For instance, to appreciate good health, one must experience bad health or sickness. To experience contentment, happiness and pleasure, one must first experience misery, pain and suffering. The same can be said about wealth and poverty, prosperity and famine, love and hate, etc. because these traits are two sides of the same coin. In other words, masculinity and femininity are the same thing expressing themselves in opposite manners. So, to indicate that Shu and Tefnut are inseparable, they were said to be brother and sister or husband and wife.

But, the Kemetic people understood that the extremities (Shu and Tefnut) of either sort are temporary and unnatural. Nature is always trying to establish a balance between these two extremes but, until that time a pendulum swings back and forth between Shu and Tefnut. The human being throws himself out of balance with nature, and intensifies the imbalance, whenever he or she refuses or resists against nature. Therefore, the purpose of life in the Kemetic philosophy was simply to conform to the way of nature. In other words, the Kemetic people believed that rather than embrace one of the traits and reject the other, it was better to seek a balance between the two. This balance is called the Maa.

As you can see, the Kemetic thinking was very different from Western and Arabic thinking because it focused on establishing balance or Maa between Shu and Tefnut. And, instead of Westerner scholars investigating the Kemetic people and their descendants, they simply relied upon their own speculations and convinced the world that their theories are true. As a result, the reason the world is no further ahead in understanding the Kemetic people is because Westerners have translated old texts – even though they do not completely understand what they are writing about.

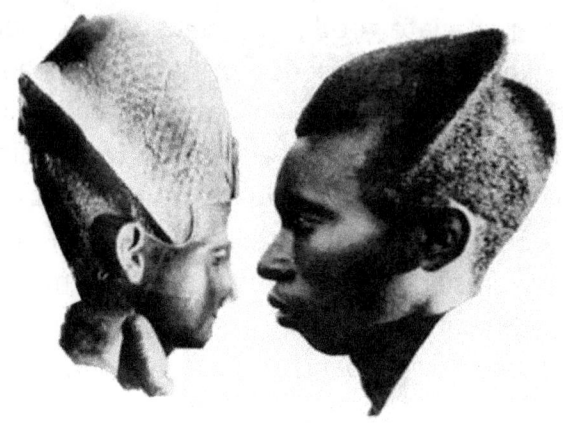

Due to this sloppy scholarship, more problems were caused and perpetuated by other "scholars" and writers who do not understand the African river-based culture.

Our best hopes of understanding of the Kemetic culture comes from accepting that the Kemetic people consists of several African ethnic groups (or tribes) who migrated throughout Sub-Sahara Africa. Once this is accepted and understood, then we can proceed to understanding how the Kemetic people lived their life and conducted their affairs because it is closely like how other indigenous Africans live throughout the Sub-Sahara.

Why Is It Important to Understand the Kemetic Philosophy?

African American have yet to define our spirituality because for years, we have been oppressed by the dominant society. Thus, African American spirituality has been called all sorts of terms including the derogatory terms hoodoo and voodoo by people who did not and were not willing to understanding it. As a result, we have yet to define what our spirituality is for ourselves, which is the reason I call it Kamta.

From this perspective, Kamta has always existed because according anthropologists every culture that has walked the earth, practiced some form of shamanism. When the Africans were kidnapped, abducted, enslaved and brought to the Americas. There were Fons and Wolofs but almost majority of the Africans shipped to North America were descendants from the Kongo-Angolan region.

A common misconception about slavery is that the Africans were forced into Christianity prior to arriving in North America. The facts are that before the advent of the slave trade, Portuguese merchants and Christian missionaries had befriended the Kongo-Angolan people around the late 15th century between the years of 1472 and 1483. Like most cultures that encounter a more technologically advanced culture, many of the Kongo-Angolan people particularly the Kongo elite, were enamored by the Portuguese culture. In 1491, the Kongo ruler, Nzinga a Nkuwu, willingly converted to Christianity and changed his name to Joao I.

To assist in this conversion, per historian John K. Thornton, missionaries used Kongo words in order to explain Christian ideas, which created a religious syncretism between the two beliefs. For instance, the missionaries used the KiKongo word "nkisi" to mean "holy" but to the Kongo people. The word "nkisi" meant medicine or charm, so church was translated to "nzo a nkisi," which is a shrine. The Bible was called "mukanda nkisi" or a charm, which to this day is still considered by many African Americans the holiest book ever created.

The spread of Christianity in the Old Kongo occurred fairly easy because besides the belief in the existence of the Supreme Being, whom they called Nzambi. The Kongo people had 1) very diverse religious beliefs, which differed from region to region, and. 2) The Kongo people did not have a large pantheon but believed that under the Supreme Being there were a host of lesser entities such as, the bakulu (ancestors), basimbi (benevolent spirits) and bankuyu (malicious woodland spirits). Consequently, Christian missionaries translated Nzambi to be the Great God of the bible, the basimbi were identified as saints, the bakulu were connected with the Christian martyrs and the bankuyu were linked with the Christian devils.

Therefore, Christianity was practiced in the Kongo-Angolan region for over a hundred years when the first Africans arrived on the shores of Jamestown, Virginia in 1619. Therefore, most if not all of the people from the Kongo-Angolan region were either Christian or at least familiar with the European faith prior to their arrival in the Americas.

When the Africans were brought to North America, the Christian teachings were perverted to make the slaves docile and obedient. Consequently, most Africans refused to convert to the new faith. This along with the fact that they were also prohibited by the slave holders to convert to religion, out of fear that the Africans would interpret the Christian message of spiritual equality with freedom, which may possibly lead to a slave revolt. Provided the foundation that encouraged the Africans to continue to practice the spiritual beliefs of their homeland. However, since the Africans in North America were separated from their homeland and thus separated from their ancestral religion. Many of them reverted to a form of African shamanism.

Thus, contrary to popular belief, the original Black Church did not meet in a building to praise God. The original Black Church met in the gullies, ravines, thickets and woods, and under wet quilts (appropriately called "hush harbors") to muffle their voices because slave owners prohibited the enslaved from praying for freedom. The original Black Church was a unique religion because it was based upon the African experience in North America, complete with an initiation system, mysticism, spiritualism, ritual complexity and the observance of certain taboos.

In the Second Great Awakening, which swept through the country from 1740 to 1780. Many Africans and African Americans converted to the Protestant Christian faith – particularly to the Baptist and Methodist denominations. However, due to the hypocrisy of slave owners, which led even the famed Frederick Douglas to note that there are two Christian religions: 1) the "pure, peaceable and impartial Christianity of Christ" and, 2) the "corrupt, slaveholding, women-whipping, cradle-plundering, partial and hypocritical Christianity of this land." Many African Americans continued to hold to their shamanistic beliefs and syncretized it with the Christianity in order to create what Thornton calls a "new Afro-Atlantic religion that was often identified as Christian, especially in the New World, but was a type of Christianity that could satisfy both African and European understanding of religion (Thornton 235).

Consequently, most of the shamans or healers in the African American community have had a unique experience in which they felt that they have been called. This calling may have been that they were born with a caul over their face. It could be that the individual survived an accident or a grave illness. Whatever the calling, the individual who has been called emerged with supernatural skills, sort-of-like a "sixth sense" that allowed them to see every aspect of the human experience as an integrated whole. This "sixth sense" is what many within the African American community referred to as one's anointing, which was only to be used to help others. If the individual chose to use their anointing for egotistical purpose and/or if the individual chose to ignore their anointing or calling for whatever reason. They would experience all sorts of hardships, obstacles, problems, and in some extreme cases death.

The healers within the African American community usually used their anointing to perform folk magick or magical acts to achieve a desired result. Folklorist Wayland Hand says in *Magical Medicine: The Folkloric Component of Medicine in the Folk Belief, Custom and Ritual of the Peoples in Europe and America* that magical acts such as pouring your woes on a letter and burning it to symbolize a transformed emotional state, performing rites at a crossroads symbolizing transition from the old to the new, tossing items over your shoulder symbolizing getting rid of a problem, walking away without looking back symbolizing relinquishing one's problem and surrendering to one's deeper mind, even the ritual act of consuming blessed wine that is believed to be magically transformed into the blood of Christ to remove sin and reconnect one back with the Christian savior, etc. are "a somewhat neglected field of folk medicine." They all work by taking an ordinary physical item and using it to symbolize a problem and through a symbolic action transforming to represents one's goal.

But over the years, the African American shamanic spiritual tradition fell into obscurity because like most folk cultures when it encounters a larger, dominant and more oppressive culture. It is being 1) obsolete and outdated by its younger constituents, therefore it is not passed down from older generations, and. 2) A spiritual practice ripe for appropriation to be used as the next great spiritual fad by members of the dominating society. Therefore, the original African American shamanic tradition is becoming more and more extinct because African Americans lost the ancestral cultural philosophy behind this rich tradition.

This combined with the negative portrayal of Africa in the media, as being a famine stricken "country" (although it is a continent with numerous countries) and African spiritual systems as being spooky, cannibalistic, demon possessing cults concerned only with placing evil curses and sticking allege victims symbolized as voodoo dolls with pins. Has caused also contributed to the flight from this tradition. Thus, many Holiness and Pentecostal religious leaders encouraged adherents to renounce the practice by considering it to be a tool of the devil; and instead put their faith in Jesus who would deliver them from evil. Out of this belief, came the cultural practice that Jesus could do anything and all practices need to be bible-based.

For example, although my parents were proud of their culture, our spiritual tradition was not openly and regularly discussed because if a practice (most likely African derived) could not be validated in the bible. It was deemed evil and it was from this understanding that blessed water was used in placed of holy water. While blessed virgin olive oil was used in place of conditioned oils. This negative attitude towards African spirituality and practice, created in my mind a serious need to understand and explain the purpose of a spiritual practice from a rational and scientific perspective. Consequently, many of the practices that exist in the church–particularly the Pentecostal churches throughout the world–such as shouting, dancing in the spirit, speaking-in-tongues, prophesizing, having visions and spirit possession (slain in the spirit), are due to African spirituality.

Although this spirituality continued to flourish for years, it began to rapidly decline between the Civil Rights, Black Power and Counterculture movements. Thus, African American spirituality got swept up in the identity politics of the era because it was alleged that African Americans being the farthest from Africa lost our culture. It was assumed that Christianity was forced upon African Americans and therefore, anyone who was practicing it, was practicing the white man's religion, which was exploitive and materialistic.

So many African Americans began searching to reclaim the inner peace, power and strength that came out of Africa with their ancestors. Consequently, anything that had to do with the church and not Black Power was abandoned in favor of religious beliefs that supported (at least on the surface) racial equality, social justice, anti-materialism (hence socialist/communist ideologies) and reflected our cultural identity. Although these perspectives were necessary, many simply threw the "baby out with the bathwater" and converted to Elijah Muhammad's Nation of Islam or, Sunni Islam inspired by Malcolm X. While many others traveled to Haiti, Cuba and/or Africa, to pay a priest or priestess to reintroduce them back to their ancestors, not knowing that their ancestors were in front of them the whole time.

However, because slavery not only shattered the lives of African descendants throughout the Afro-Diaspora but also devastated many African people living on the continent. Some African Americans turned instead to Kemet (Ancient Egypt, which is believed to be the Motherland of African spirituality) because Kemet is believed to have a more unadulterated form of African spirituality.

Initially, inspired by the rising interest in Afrocentricity and supported by the understanding that the Kemetic people were black and brown Africans according to the father of Western history, Herodotus, who gives a detailed description of the Kemetic, and. W.E.B. DuBois, Chiekh Anta Diop, George G.M. James, Carter G. Woodson, J.A. Rogers, Chancellor Williams, Arturo Alfonso Schomburg, John Henrik Clarke, Gerald Massey, Godfrey Higgins, T. Obenga, Ivan van Sertima, Yosef Alfredo Antonio Ben-Jochannan, Molefi Kete Asante, Leonard Jefferies, Anthony Browder and many more. Many people simply imitated the Kemetic culture based upon Western scholarship. While many others simply focused on the historical accomplishments of the Kemetic society. However, a small few chose to focus on the cultural similarities of the Kemetic people with ancient and contemporary traditional African societies. Many of these Kemetic inspired spiritual systems syncretized the Kemetic beliefs with existing African and African derived traditions. That anyone can practice regardless of their religious affiliation, beliefs or background because it officially has no rules.

However, today what some of us, such as myself, have found is that for us to move forward spiritually. We must understand how our ancestors survived slavery using Christianity. This means we really need to get over our protest of the church's trappings and realize that our ancestors converted to Christianity to preserve their spiritual culture and tradition. In other words, elements of the Christian myth were adopted to preserve their cultural way of life, which is the reason the Moses and the Exodus of the Children of Israel was such a popular theme.

Once I separated the various scandals and other negative components of the church and understood the reasons our ancestors practiced their beliefs in the gullies, ravines, thickets, woods, and under wet quilts. I found that the real reason slave owners prohibited the Africans and early African Americans from praying—which thankfully they continued to do—was because our ancestors entered an altered state of consciousness, for all their needs. In other words, early African Americans did not result to using their spirituality or calling upon God as a "last resort." They called upon God (and any other force) they could conjure to help them to improve their lot all the time.

Our ancestors prayed to God (and to their ancestors) for anything and for everything. They basically prayed so much that it became a cultural tradition for us to "Put God first" in everything we do in our life. Thus, to this day African Americans always begin everything by first thanking God who is recognized as the Source. Since African American spirituality has fostered a type of "sixth sense," which includes the belief in spirits or at least the survival of the soul. It is not uncommon to find in many African American churches, photos of deceased elders (usually dressed in white) in a place of honor, which is a Creolized version of ancestor veneration. Even African American youth practice a form of ancestor veneration by pouring libations (usually liquor) for friends no longer physically alive. Clearly, African culture was not lost due to slavery, but the philosophy and theology behind our cultural practices were.

As a result, thanks to Sir E. A. Wallis Budge who staunchly disagreed with his colleagues and published in *Osiris: The Egyptian Religion Of Resurrection,* that the ancient Egyptians were (and had always been) Black Africans based upon cultural comparisons with Africans who lived in the Congo, Niger, Sudan, Tanganyika, Nigeria, and Ghana and throughout Sub-Sahara Africa by syncretizing the remnants of the Bantu-Kongo beliefs that survived in North America with the Kemetic philosophy. Kamta was created to make the Kemetic philosophy practical and applicable.

How to Practice Kamta?

The BA, Ab and sahu

The basis of Kamta stems around the understanding of the sahu, Ab and BA:

The sahu is the subconscious part of our being that is often referred to as the animal-self, the physical body awareness, and the lower self because its' sole purpose to help us to physically survive. It corresponds to the oldest part of the human brain known as the R-complex or reptilian brain.

The Ab is the self-conscious part of our being that is often referred to as the Conscious, the Spiritual Heart and/or the Soul. The Ab is responsible for changing and directing the programming of the BA and sahu.

The BA is the Superconscious part of our being that is often referred to as the God-self, the Divine Spark, the Higher Self or our personal Guardian Angel. The BA is the artist and one can connect to it through meditation and rituals, like working with the netcharu (guardian spirits). The BA is symbolized as a human headed hawk because it rests on our head and is the wisest part of our being.

The Rau

At the heart of the Kemetic philosophy is a concept called Ra or Rau (plural). Rau is like the aura but it is more than that. Rau is the divine power, the chi, the life force, the Holy Ghost, the spiritual power that exists all around us and in all things.

When the Perfect Creator, Nebertchar – the Lord of All Things – created the Universe, after self-creating Itself and creating Maa (Divine Balance and Order), brought the Ra into existence, so everything – plants, animals, rocks, rivers, oceans, mountains, human beings, ancestors, even words such as poems and curses – depend on Ra because it is a breathing, living and palpable flow of energy. That passes through us, is constantly used by us and must be replenished by us for there to be balance or Maa.

Every being has its own Rau or ra (personal spiritual power), which is not to be understood as dominion over another but, the spiritual power to produce change and make things happen.

Human beings can access their ra through their BA, which means that only human beings can increase or decrease his or her ra power through diligent application of honorable and noble deeds, calm and proactive behavior such as offerings and rituals. For this reason, to remind us of this divine ability, the Kemetic sages commonly symbolized Rau as a hawk headed man with a coiled cobra around a solar disk resting on his head. To indicate that the secrets to managing one's ra and unlocking your mind power. Rests not in finding inner peace or becoming "one with everything" but rather in shutting down all secondary thoughts.

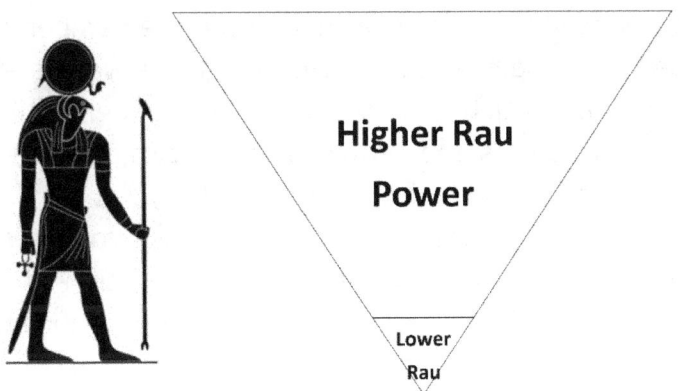

focus your brain's processing power on a singular point or action, hence enter an altered state of consciousness or a deep state of trance. In other words, disciplining one's mind by learning how to consciously ignore images, feelings, thoughts, voices, music, etc. at will, that both the BA (Superconscious) and sahu (subconscious) will bring to your awareness.

What separates gods and goddesses from men and women, is that the former has acquired power by disciplining him or herself, while the latter has not, hence the reason we are here. More will be said about this in detail, in Part Two of this book. For now, it is important to understand that there is only Rau Power and the more Rau power (more Spiritual Light) one acquires the more powerful they become, and they can utilize their higher mental abilities. While the less Rau power (Less Spiritual Light or Spiritual Darkness) one has and the more they rely upon their basic instincts.

Spiritual Development

Therefore, spiritual development has nothing to do with being good or bad. It is about learning how to discipline one's mind to acquire more Rau power. From the Kemetic perspective, one of the reasons our current societies are collapsing is not because there are not enough good people in the world. It is because there is a severe shortage of spiritual power. I remember, when I used to be in sales selling security systems, there was a statistic we used to quote, which was that 90% of people believe in doing good, but when these same people are put into a dire circumstance and compromising situation. They will break the law. In other words, most people know that it is wrong to steal but, if you put a desperately hungry man in a situation where he can steal food, he will. Why? It is simply because his hunger has consumed his rational thinking. It has nothing to do with his morals. The real question(s) is why is he hungry? How did this individual get into this predicament? If we fix what got him into this situation in the first place, we not only have prevented an individual from being incarcerated because they had no food to eat. We also have improved society by investing in the mental and spiritual wellbeing of this individual.

This is what Kemetic shamanism focuses on. No, it is not about being "good" because good people get taken advantage of all of the time. We hear and see it on the radio, TV, Internet, etc. The world is full of good people. In fact, there is an unlimited amount of good people. What the world lacks is powerful people. There is a limited amount of power.

So, the Kemetic tradition focuses upon disciplining one's mind in order to acquire more Rau power. The more one's mind is disciplined, the more ra power they can acquire and use to make things happen. To help us in acquiring more ra power we work with two spiritual beings: the netcharu (guardian spirits) and aakhu (ancestors and spirit guides).

The netcharu are believed to be the first individuals to have disciplined their mind and acquired ra power. Below is a listing of the netcharu from the most disciplined to the least disciple:

- Osar, the Lord of the Underworld, owner of the white Hedjet crown and arbiter of justice, uses his ra to increase one's knowledge and clarity.
- Djahuti uses his ra to increase one's wisdom (the ability to solve problems peacefully) via dreams and prophecy.
- Sokar uses his ra power to improve one's health, helps one to overcome illness and blesses one with the power of resilience, persistence and the power of rebirth/renewal.
- Maat uses her ra to establish balance and order where there is none. She also helps uses her ra to help the righteous, truth seekers, those struggling with legal issues and wealth matters.
- Hru Aakhuti used his ra to create tools, weapons and fight against injustice. Consequently, he uses his ra to assist those in finding employment and in helping those who need brute force to accomplish physical demanding tasks. He also uses his ra to protect the deserving (especially those involved in activities regarding metals, tools and weapons), to help people learn the difference between courage and cowardice, as well as muster the inner strength to live righteously no matter how difficult it may be.
- Hru, the true heir of Osar and Oset, uses his ra power to help people to use their power for productive purposes, including defeating an oppressor and succeeding in achieving their goals.
- Nebhet uses her ra to create love, romance, and to attract money and help couples conceive.
- Npu (Anubis) is the most famous netchar because he reminds us of the success (or failure) due to our beliefs/thoughts that comes when we take control of our destiny. He uses his ra to open the doors to what we want such as love, money, luck, general health, etc. but cautions us to be careful of what we ask for.

- Oset uses her ra to bless one mothers with a successful and healthy pregnancy. She also uses her ra to assist all mothers and families in providing for all their needs.
- Set although not honored, is the youngest brother of Osar and considered to be the most undisciplined netchar, and therefore the one with the least amount of ra power. He is a constant reminder of the consequences of having an undisciplined mind and failure to take control over one's destiny resulting in chaos, confusion, calamity and disorder.

In addition to working with the netcharu, we also have the:

- Aakhu – benevolent ancestral spirits and spirit guides use their ra power to assist their loved ones, living descendants and other family members in all family matters. The aakhu are not just RNA or DNA but in fact energy and wisdom of our deceased loved ones. The aakhu exist because the essence of who we are– energy–and energy cannot be created or destroyed, so when a person dies. Their essence or soul continues to exist after death as energy and wisdom, and is accessible to those who venerate the dead. For instance, if you had a relative who died because of preventable health condition. Now that they can see how they made their mistakes while living, they can help you so that you do not make the same errors regarding your health.
- Aapepu – malevolent, confused, misguided ancestral and trickster spirits who have a very small amount of ra power, so they use it to trick the living into wasting their ra power as they did.

Per ancient African beliefs, since the netcharu are within us and exist throughout nature, whenever we need their assistance. By calling on them we can take the small amount of the netcharu within us and tie it with its energy in nature. Therefore, an individual desiring better relation between himself and his wife may be encouraged to petition Nebhet, the netchart of love, romance, money and conception. After which Nebhet assists in resolving the relationship issues. A candle, honey, fruit and/or money is offered as payment to Nebhet in exchange for her ra to fix the relationship between the husband and wife.

Now, some people may feel uncomfortable with the idea of making offerings or paying a spirit for a blessing. But this is a very shamanistic approach that has been used for ages, all over the world, in everything from healing rites to the erection of a building. It is Maa (Balance) and it is a reminder that you do not get something from nothing. Therefore, the relationship between the living and the Spirits (aakhu and netcharu) is quid pro quo, which roughly means "you give me something, in exchange for something."

The reason archeologists, historians, scientists, theologians, etc. have not been able to comprehend how this work is because they do not understand that there are some problems that our rational mind cannot solve but must be resolved intuitively. The same way one would pray to God for deliverance and has faith their prayer will be answered; is the same way one petitions the aakhu and netcharu. However, the difference is that faith alone is not enough to create the change needed. If it were, many god-fearing people based upon their belief in God would have better lives free of addictions. Permanent change requires that one also use their ra, which is why offerings are made. However, working with the netcharu and aakhu could not yield any true spiritual progress without divination.

Divination

Divination is not used to predict the future, but to inform us of what would occur if we choose to be reactive instead of proactive. In other words, divination is used to inform us what is most likely to occur if we do not do anything to change a current situation. There are many forms of divination that are and can be used including dreams, visions, omens, signs and oracles. For more information on simple and easy to use oracle, without all the religious dogma associated with divination, see *Maa: A Guide to the Kemetic Way for Personal Transformation*.

Attuning Your Energy through Holistic Living

Finally, it is very important that to progress spiritually, you should attune your energy adopting a holistic lifestyle. Before we begin, we must recognize that the reason most diets fail is not because they do not work. Most diets fail because most people do not understand what a lifestyle change means. For instance, if you decide to go on a high protein-low complex carbohydrate diet. You need to be prepared to do this for the rest of your life. If you decide to exercise 30 minutes to an hour a day to be healthier, then this means you must prepare to do this for the rest of your life. This is what a lifestyle change means but most people when they go on a diet, only do it for a specific time frame and this is the reason it does not work.

To live holistically, you have to be committed to living this way for the rest of your life. This is the reason I do not promote any type of lifestyle such as a vegan and vegetarian lifestyle because if vegan or vegetarian finds themselves in a food desert where they cannot get an adequate amount of produce and vegetable proteins. Many vegans and vegetarians will consume junk food (potato chips, chocolate, etc.) all because it is still vegetable. I have known many vegetarians and vegans who were unhealthier than meat eaters because they did not understand what holistic lifestyle means.

So, holistic first and foremost means listening to your body's needs. For some, they may need to consume more vegetables, for others they may need to consume more proteins, while others may need to do both as well as exercise, do meditative exercises and meditate, and so on.

Now, contrary to popular belief, holistic living does not mean becoming a vegetarian or vegan. By the way, you do not have to be a vegetarian or vegan to be spiritual. Another misnomer is that human beings are not natural herbivores (vegetarians) or carnivores (meat eaters), but omnivores. This basically means that human beings can survive eating plants or animals. If you follow the evolution of our species, human beings had to adapt to all types of climatic differences, which is why human beings can be found to this day consuming everything. So, let's discuss cuisines.

In my personal research, as I overcame my dis-ease, I learned that it is a myth that the African American diet was a very poor diet due to slavery. Slaves were considered a commodity. No, the enslaved Africans did not have the best quality food but it was not worse. Slave owners per Dr. Frederick Opie, author of *Hogs and Hominy: Soul Food from Africa to the Americas*, tried to reproduce African foodstuffs in the cheapest manner possible. The poorest quality of food could not provide the nourishment or energy needed for people who burned on an average 2000+ calories a day. In other words, the slave owners had to give the enslaved Africans decent provisions to ensure that they were healthy to work the plantations. In some regions, the enslaved Africans could have plots of land to grow their own food, while others were given certain provisions and supplemented their diet by hunting and fishing. Slaves were responsible for providing food everyone including themselves and their slave owners.

The problem with the present African American diet or "Soul Food" is: 1) that it is not cooked by our hands. It is processed from big food companies, which means it consists of a host of additives, chemicals and other ingredients, and. 2) too many celebratory meals are eaten in excesses. For instance, back in the day, Grandma did not cook macaroni and cheese, chitterlings, stuffing, rolls, sweet potato pie, etc. every day. This was cooked and consumed on special occasions, once or three times out of the year because good soul food, like most good tasting food, is time consuming to prepare.

When African Americans migrated from the south to escape the white terrorist group known as the ku klux klan. They abandoned a lot of their agricultural ways as the succeeding generations continued to dwell in the cities. For instance, I fondly remember my grandparents and other in their generation having gardens, raising their own livestock and regularly going to the farmer's market. I remember out of my parents' generation; my parents were the only ones among their friends that had a garden. Most got their food from the super convenient grocery stores and this is how many began eating processed foods. It all began out of convenience and therefore there are so many fast food restaurants in our communities to this day.

You know the statistics, hypertension, cardiac arrest, diabetes and many other preventable dis-eases are on the rise in our community, but it can all be turned around by adopting a holistic lifestyle that addresses the needs of our mind, body and soul. This is the reason it is important that we learn the true history of our dietary downfall and not the myths, so that we can address the problem.

When I began to understand that the two reasons our diet plunged, I learned that one of the main reasons why many of these preventable ill-nesses exist so prevalent in our community, is because our diets are rich in complex carbohydrates and is protein deficient. This is a cultural problem and not a dietary one. I remember when I was a vegetarian, when other vegetarians and vegans could not get a decent meal. They would result to eating potato chips, pasta, rice, chocolate and processed foods without meat because "it is not meat," which would spike their sugar. A couple of these people are now vegetarian diabetics.

When I changed my diet due to lupus, I made it a rule to stay away from the inside aisles of a grocery store because this is where most processed foods are stored. In other words, I stay on the outside aisles of the store and get my produce, lean meats, seafood, etc. and then I am out of the store. The only time I go in the middle is to get frozen vegetables when the fresh vegetable is not available.

I do not exercise every day because I live a pretty active life. When I was sedentary, I would try to walk for 30 minutes a day and get some weight lifting in to fit my schedule. The point is that you must start somewhere and when you do. All you need to do is make it a part of your life. Everything does not work for everyone. For instance, I have heard people say that they juice vegetables because they do not like to eat them all the time. Whatever works go for it. The one thing is, you should not feel stressed or burdened. Here's some suggestions. Note that this information is not used diagnosed:

Diet: Ideally, a well-balanced diet should consist of a protein (legumes or lean meats like poultry and/or fish), carbohydrates (vegetables, whole grains, and fruits), fat (olive oil, coconut oil, palm oil, peanut oil, etc.) and plenty of water. Note that if you are craving sugar, constantly becoming sick, feeling weak, experiencing hair loss, it may signify a protein deficiency. It is recommended that you consume 2000 calories then you should be consuming between 50 to 150 grams of protein because undereating is just as bad as overeating.

To ensure that your body gets the necessary nutrients, breakfast should be 85% protein, 10% carbohydrates and 5% fat. If this suggestion is followed, you should not be hungry until the afternoon. In this case, a similar meal but lighter should be consumed. Dinner should be light consisting of maybe a soup or salad. The mantra for this dietary lifestyle is *"Eat breakfast like king, lunch like a prince and dinner like a pauper."*

Although fruit is natural, it is still composed of fructose sugar and an excessive amount of sugar contributes to illness. Naturally, fruit is usually seasonal, but the food industry has made it possible for us to get fruit from all over the world out of season. This is not holistic. There is a reason watermelon grows in abundant during the summer months and not the winter months. It is suggested that fruit should be consumed once a day no more than three pieces a day. The best fruit to consume all year around due to its fiber content are apples, but again. This is my opinion.

The thing is, people have made dietary lifestyle a religion. No one should feel as if the Divine is going to punish them and send them to hell because they ate a food off the Judeo-Christian-Muslim food list. This is why I say; you have to decide what is best for you by simply listening to what your body needs in order to maintain optimal health. To evaluate your progress, journal your food and exercise experiences, thoughts and actions. You might want to include the date, time of the day, time of the year and season, when you ate, exercise, etc.

Disclaimer: This information is intended to be educational and not for diagnosis, prescription, or treatment of any health disorder whatsoever. This information should not replace consultation with a competent healthcare professional. The content of the book is intended to be used as an adjunct to a rational and responsible healthcare program prescribed by a licensed healthcare practitioner. This is a book about faith. As such the author and publisher do not warrant the success any person would have using any of the exercises and techniques contained herein. Success and failure will vary. The author and publisher therefore are in no way liable for any misuse of the material contained herein.

Lesson One: Preparing for Spiritual Exchange

The following are exercises and techniques that will be used in your development and practice.

Meditation & Prayer

We do not meditate to merge our consciousness with the Great Divine to achieve enlightenment because there is no applicable use for it. Enlightenment does not pay our bills, put food on our table, place a roof over our head, clothe our children, etc. We do not concentrate on believing in the Divine. We concern ourselves with knowing who the Divine is by praying (sending a request) and meditating (listening for a response) to our problems.

To Pray:
1. Simply express your gratitude for everything you are grateful for. Then, ask for help revolving an issue.
2. I have found that most people believe their prayers are not answered because they obsess over the results. Therefore, I suggest focusing only on the question. Then, do something to get your mind off the subject like take a shower, wash dishes, watch TV, do laundry, etc. Usually performing chores allows your mind to focus on a present issue, thus making you receptive to hearing a solution to your prayer.

To Meditate:
1. All that is required is that you relax your body and allow your mind to run free. Do not focus on any idea or thought that enters your awareness. Simply ignore them. The more you practice this exercise the more relax you will become, the slower to anger and the less likely to be influenced by others.

2. Say "Thank you" knowing that a solution is coming.

Special Movements to Manipulate Energy

To manipulate how energy flow certain gestures can be used to place protective energy within things and to expel energy. For instance, many spiritual healers will cleanse their home by burning a heavy incense and opening all the windows or use a brand-new broom to beat the walls with a strong fragrant herbal bath, both gestures are done to symbolize chasing energy out of the dwelling. Another common gesture is the throwing of objects you want to forget over your left shoulder into a running stream. To make use of special movements it is best that you familiarize yourself with your own gestures and symbolic meanings. Observe your daily routines, your actions and how you go about doing things.

Here are a few common gestures that will be used throughout this book:

- Knocking three times on the floor, altar or imaginary crossroad of the maa aankh (covered in the next chapter) to open the door to the spiritual realm or KAMTA.
- Since things grow from bottom up, to attract something to you move from feet to the head. To remove something move from head to feet.
- To bless candles to attract something anoint from base to wick. To repel turn candle upside down and bite or break the wick end. Then anoint from the old wick to the base. Light the base end.
- Folding arms and crossing legs is a gesture symbolizing closing oneself off from receiving energy.
- Negative energy can be dispelled by suddenly clapping your hands three times while calling upon the spirits aloud.
- Positive spirits are believed to rest on the right shoulder, while negative spirits parade on the left (more will be said

about this in the future). This is the meaning behind throwing salt over your left shoulder.
- Disposing of ritual items and/or offerings and not looking back symbolizes putting a matter in your Superconscious/Spirits hands.
- Sucking and pulling motions with your hands are used to draw energy out of something.
- Cutting and hacking movements are used to cut binds.

There are many others and you are free to incorporate your own. The most widely used special movement in this book is the drawing of the maa aankh discussed in the Lesson Two.

Chanting & Tarrying

I remember when I was younger and I went to church, to get the Holy Ghost we were told to repeat the words "Hallelujah" and/or "Jesus" until the Holy Ghost (mediumistic trance state) fell on us. They called it *tarrying for the Spirit*. I remember being told that the reason this works was because of the "power in the name of Jesus." Later, as I learned more about the BA (Superconscious) and sahu (subconscious), I found that anything repeated causes the sahu to go into autopilot and gives us access to our BA. In other words, any word or name said repetitively can lead to an altered state of consciousness. However, some words are better at producing a trance state because they are based upon sound. For instance, the power in Hallelujah is the "jah," which is the reason Rastafarians favored this as the name of God but, any name can be used. Amen is such a popular term that ends Jewish, Christian and Muslim prayers because when you chant Amen or AMN it is like chanting OM. To chant or tarry:
1. Inhale deeply,
2. Say AMEN or AMN slowly to yourself, sounding each letter, as you exhale.
3. Repeat.

Remember, this can be done for any of the netcharu. Also, it can be done aloud as well. This practice works well when combined with meditation exercises.

Rituals

A ritual is basically an organized ceremony to achieve a desired result of either planting positive energy or removing negative energy. A shamanic ritual may include prayer, meditation, special movements along with numerous items. Rituals are typically performed once a day, week, month and/or annually. There are numerous rituals that can be performed because shamanism focuses on maintaining and/or restoring wholeness. All rituals should be planned in the beginning. Rituals should always begin with a prayer to incorporate assistance from your Spirits. Followed by a prayer of what you specifically want to accomplish. Next, follow your intuition. Please note that benevolent spirits will never inspire you to compromise your principles by harm yourself or others. Finally, close the ritual by saying thanks.

For instance, a simple house cleansing ritual involves pouring a cap of ammonia, a cap of vinegar, and a Florida Water into a bucket of water. Take a new mop and mop the corners from top to bottom to remove negative influences. Make sure that you move in a clockwise direction towards your front door, as if chasing someone out of your home. Flush the mop water in the toilet. Afterwards, moving in a counter clockwise motion beginning with the front door, sprinkle or spray fragrances in your corner from the floor to the ceiling. For instance, cinnamon for love and money, lavender for tranquility, etc.

Offerings

Human beings have a bad habit of abusing, misusing and neglecting anything that is freely received and not earned, which in Part Two, of this book, we will discuss why from a Kemetic perspective. To trump this negative habit, it is a good gesture that every time you ask for something you make an offering. Anything can be offered such as candles, water, fruit, no salted food, coins, etc. Rest assure, you do not have to offer your soul or your first born. Contrary to the horror movies, Spirits do not want this. They want out of anything, time and energy. Therefore, get in the habit of making offerings because it is a good way to stay in alignment with the Universe.

Fasting or Sacrificing

Although ascetics have made fasting to be an extreme spiritual practice. The purpose of fasting is to make a sacrifice. A sacrifice means that you give up something physical in return for something spiritual blessing. We fast for various reasons. For instance, if a person truly wants to lose excessive fat, it is suggested that they fast on sugar and carbohydrates for a period. During this time, their Spirits will give them insight on how to accomplish their goal. To improve relations between you and someone. Fast to not get angry while talking with them.

Fasting usually requires giving up something that you are in the habit of doing. You can fast on food, drink, sex, actions, behaviors, television or any activity. You can even fast by saying that every time you do something you will give up money, such as a swear jar but instead of a dollar. Try giving up five dollars. Again, the psycho-spiritual purpose is that you are sacrificing something you like and enjoy for something you need.

To effectively fast (or sacrifice):
1. Write a list of all the things that you like and enjoy.
2. Choose one thing from the list that you are willing to give up for the sake of a goal. Hint: The hardest thing to give up is usually the thing that will give you the most power towards achieving your goal.

3. State "I will give up _____."
4. State, "In return assist (or bless) me with (name problem)."

Continue to fast until you achieve your goal. Of course, if you are fasting from food, be sure to check with your physician.

Affirmations, Declarations, Glyphs and Sigils

I am going to make this section short and sweet because there is a growing group of people that comes from a strong religious background trying to convince people that the *42 Laws of Maat* should be committed to memory, recited and followed like the *Ten Commandments*. This is totally untrue. The *42 Laws of Maat* are declarations, which is a powerful that you emphatically say aloud. Unlike affirmations, which state that a goal has already happened, which your sahu (subconscious) fights against because it feels true.

A declaration sends a powerful message to the universe and your BA (Superconscious) and sahu part of your being of a goal you want to achieve. In other words, most affirmations do not work because they lack feeling and without feeling, it is difficult to convince your sahu to assist you. Declarations are a better choice, but the problem with reciting *42 Laws of Maat* is that we do not live in ancient Kemet, so many of these declarations are irrelevant. Remember, the Kemetic people were an agrarian society. Most of us today do not even know how to grow garlic, not to mention anything else that is agriculturally related. So, we need a new set of declarations that will assist us in this lifetime. We need declarations that will help us with overindulgence, which is contributing to hypertension, obesity, diabetes, etc. e.g. "I have not overindulged in the consumption of fruit," which most people do not understand also that fructose (sugar found in fruit) also contributes to excessive amount of sugar in our body, even though it is natural. This is the reason it is futile to recite the *42*

Laws of Maat because unless you are saying them aloud in front of group of people who care about your spiritual development. It is not invoking the response needed to produce change. A better option is to use glyphs or sigils.

Glyphs or sigils are basically ideas that have been transformed into graphic symbols. Think hieroglyphs and you will understand that meaning behind the saying that "a picture is worth a thousand words." The science behind this is that both the BA and sahu do not communicate in words but in symbols. This is the reason smokers who want to quit their habit are not successful when they tell their BA and/or sahu "I want to quit smoking" or break some other destructive habit. The message is never conveyed to BA and sahu because they do not speak English, Spanish, French, etc. They speak symbols and specifically symbols that generate strong emotions or will jolt your spirit. The best symbols for the job are sigils.

There are a lot of ways to make sigils and everyone has a method that works for them. I stumbled upon this method while studying how to influence my own lower self (sahu). Later, I found that some other authors have come to the same conclusion, which was verification to me that I was in sync with the times. The traditional way to make sigils is by first writing a statement of intent such as, "I will have top sales this year." Then you would cancel all the vowels and the repeating consonants, then make a glyph or sigil out of the remaining letters.

Instead of affirming, I suggest asking a question instead as if the goal was already achieved. For instance, instead of "I will have top sales this year." I would write, "How did my sales become so high this year?"

First, I cross out the vowels. The interesting thing is that many of the Kemetic words do not have vowels. Now, sometimes I cross out the Y because it is pronounced as a vowel, but other times I may leave it.

> HOW DID MY SALES BECOME SO HIGH THIS YEAR?

> H~~O~~W D~~I~~D M~~Y~~ SAL~~E~~S B~~E~~C~~O~~ME S~~O~~ H~~I~~GH TH~~I~~S Y~~E~~AR?

Second, I cross out repeating consonants.

> HW DD M SLS BCM S HGH THS YR?

> HW D~~D~~ M SLS BCM ~~S~~ ~~H~~GH T~~HS~~ YR?

Third, I take the remaining letters and make a glyph or sigil.

> HW D M SL BCM G T YR?

Finally, I try to make it as aesthetically appealing as possible. The idea is to totally lose sight that this is your wish.

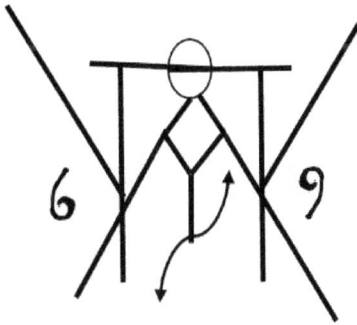

Once I have a clear image of the glyph or sigil, then I send it to my BA and sahu by going into trance. Understand, the science behind this technique is that when an image is firmly impressed upon our sahu. When the sahu realizes that it cannot do anything with it. It will hand it over to your BA, which is connected to the universal Rau power.

There are several ways you can enter into a trance state such as through meditating, chanting, fasting, dancing around for hours until you become exhausted, using illicit drugs (which is common in many shamanic societies), sex and masturbation. However, let me explain why I favor the last option over all the rest.

Meditation, chanting, dancing until you are completely exhausted and fasting take an enormous amount of time to help you enter a trance state. For the record, they are effective but personally I find meditating, dancing around for hours, chanting or fasting for hours or days, for boost in sales, a little ridiculous.

Although many shamanic societies use drugs like Yohimbe, marijuana, alcohol, etc. to help facilitate a trance state. These people have a different cultural appreciation and understanding for herbal drugs than those of us living in instant gratifying Western societies. When drugs are used in the West, most focus on the effect and not the intent, which results in them becoming sleepy, dim-witted, hyperactive, loopy and distracted from their objective. This is the reason; I strongly advise against using any drugs of any kind for spiritual purposes.

Sex and masturbation are safer choices because they are better controlled but, unless your partner is willing to assist you in firing your glyph or sigil. I recommend that sexual intercourse be used only by husband and wife because they are committed to each other's development (or should be). They will help each remember the purpose of the ritual, then one-night stands. This is because the union between husband and wife is not just for procreation but spiritual creation between masculine and feminine forces (Shu and Tefnut, Geb and Nut, Yang and Yin, etc.).

That being said, masturbation is safer and better choice for assisting in trance for firing glyphs and sigils because you are able to exercise more control and discipline.

Finally, to fire the glyph or sigil off, once you achieve orgasm, stare at the glyph or sigil. Drink it into your mind, then immediately forget about it. The easiest way to forget about the glyph or sigil is by going to do something else like washing dishes, watching TV, exercising, etc. The reason for not thinking about the glyph or sigil is that leads you to worry, which will cause you to become anxious and wonder when your desire will manifest. You must remember that your BA knows what your sahu does not, which is the reason for doing this little ritual in the first place. So, do not fret about your goal, let your BA do what it was designed to do.

Now, I must say that using masturbation for this purpose transforms it from teenage debauchery to a higher purpose. In fact, most "spiritual people" would not mention it because of the taboo associated with it. But, if you have any hang-ups with masturbation because of your religious upbringing, I would suggest that you visit a reputable psychological health website and learn about the myths and truths about masturbation. If after visiting these sites you still have hang-ups regarding masturbation, then use the meditation, chanting, or try dancing for hours to impress your glyph or sigil unto your Ba and sahu.

I have personally found that creating glyphs or sigils is best for anything that involves developing your character and improving your mind, body and soul.

I have yet to find any success for using this technique in winning the lottery or coming into any sum of money. Understand, that this does not mean that it does not exist. I just personally have not found it to work for me. It just doesn't seem to work because most people have a lot of hang-ups in regard to money. If they were born with money, they think that they are entitled to get money, and if they are born without a lot of money, they think it is evil.

So, do not create glyphs or sigils for money unless you have serious time to explore and reprogram your sahu in regard to money. Instead, use the glyphs and sigils to overcome negative habits, help in developing new habits, and improving your character like managing your temper. Also, you cannot use these to influence others, but you can use it to affect how you react. For instance, "Why is my wife so kind and loving to me these days?" This allows your BA to transform how you respond to your spouse, which will entail influence how she acts towards you.

For the record, it is not necessary for you to learn the sesh metu (Kemetic hieroglyphs) because we each have a plethora of symbols within our mind. This combined with other cultures we have all encounter adds more symbols that we can use, so there is no real purpose for using the hieroglyphs because it is obsolete. It is like the Latin language, a great reference point but no one speaks it. It is better for you to develop your own glyphs and sigils, then focus on symbols that were used a thousand years ago, because your creation has more significance now.

Recognizing Signs

It is recommended that you jot down your experience and pay attention to:

- Your Dreams – Dreams can reveal that you are on a spiritual path. To interpret your dreams simply question how certain events and/or symbols made you feel.
- Number Sequences (Numerology) – you will notice that certain numbers (and number sequences) will

appear on a regular basis in your life. These are a sign that a certain guardian spirit is governing this area of your life. For instance, sometimes I wake up and look at my alarm clock, which reads 3:00 AM. The number 3 is Npu's number and it is an indicator that he is on the job. See appendix for numerology rules.
- Omens – Omens are defined as an "occurrence or phenomenon believed to foretell a future event. In other words, omens are strange signs that have no rational explanation but signify that if we continue to follow our current choice something either positive or negative is going to happen. Certain spirits have colors, animal totems, gems, metals, etc.
- Synchronous Events – Synchronicity is defined by Merriam-Webster as "coincidental occurrence of events and especially psychic events (as similar thoughts in widely separated persons or a mental image of an unexpected event before it happens) that seem related but are not explained by conventional mechanisms of causality —used especially in the psychology of C. G. Jung[1]." In other words, coincidences do not happen. The people you meet, the friends you make, the enemies whose paths you cross, etc. all have a purpose and are trying to reveal something to you, and.
- Your Talents – Talents/Skills are any mental or intellectual aptitude that you may have is an indication that a guardian spirit has taken a liking towards you and will be assisting you on your spiritual path.

---

[1] Synchronicity. (2017). In *MerriamWebesterDictionaries.com*. Retrieved from https://www.merriam-webster.com/dictionary/synchronicity

TWO:
Finding Your Maa Aankh

I gave up on Christianity a long time ago because 1) my parents' church refused to take a stand against the crack-cocaine violence that was claiming the youth in Detroit, and. 2) Every problem had the same remedy, pray, give your life to Jesus, and you will be saved.

But, after giving my life to Jesus and failing. I, "backslid" and was convinced thereafter, that I was not one of the chosen few selected to go to heaven when I die. I simply believed that God did not want me so, even though I still believed in God. I grew very distant from God whom I saw as a tyrannical deity like the Greek Zeus.

Stunned, disappointed and depressed, I contemplated suicide so that I could cuss God out in the hereafter. Then, ask him why he made it so difficult for Black people to live, and did not give us any way for us to get out of the situation. That's when a voice spoke to me and inspired me to study the Kemetic religion.

So, for years I read and studied everything that I could find about the Kemetic people and their spiritual way of life. Then, I met a "spiritual teacher" who claimed to have had all of this spiritual knowledge and experience. Being young and naïve, I followed this individual because I had no internal reference to compare what they were telling me with. As a result, my blind obedience resulted in me being unemployed and for a few years homeless, but after following this individual and realizing that they were a charlatan. I began to give up on Kemetic spirituality all together, until I met Papa.
Papa was an elderly Black Cuban who was a high priest called a Babalawo in Lukumi (also known as Santeria), a practicing spiritist

(as many in Lukumi are) and a member of the all-male Abakua Society. In my previous works, I have written a lot about how I admired this man because in the short time I knew him, this Child of the Orisha Ellegua, gave me so much direction, so I will not discuss it here. However, the most memorable experience I had with Papa is when he learned that I was mimicking the Kemetic religion and he scolded me. He told me in so many words that it was foolish to imitate the way of life of a people who was not living the way I was living in these contemporary times. He told me instead to focus on the concepts and principles because all African religions have the same roots.

Shortly after giving me that wise advice, I lost contact with Papa, but he told me what I needed to gather the courage to leave my "spiritual teacher." When I left, I returned back to my parents' home. Feeling like a prodigal son, I tried to ween myself off of Kemetic spirituality and spiritual traditions in its entirety. I was strongly contemplating being agnostic but I had too many experiences that convinced me that spirits were real. They were just not real for me so I began to focus on my career and spent years trying to amass wealth.

Then one day everything changed and I became gravely ill. Due to my illness, I was unable to work. I was already living paycheck-to-paycheck prior to becoming ill, so I did not know how I was going to survive. Then, one day my younger brother told me that "You're going to have to work your faith" but I did not have any faith.

Then, while I was ill, I learned about an African symbol that was brought to the Americas from Central Africa during the slavery. This symbol or cosmogram known as the *dikenga dia Kongo* or *tendwa kia nza-n' Kongo* (in KiKongo) was commonly called the Kongo Cross.

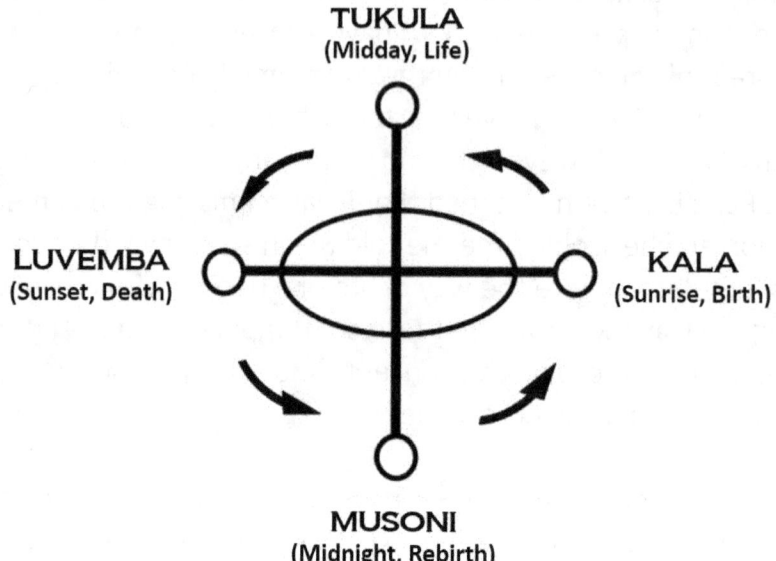

The Kongo Cross has nothing to do with the Christian Cross but its meaning overlaps the Christian concepts. The general understanding of the sign is that soul like the sun rises (Kala), peaks at midday (Tukula), sets at sunset (Luvemba) and is reborn as midnight (MusonI), thus revealing the indestructibility of the soul.

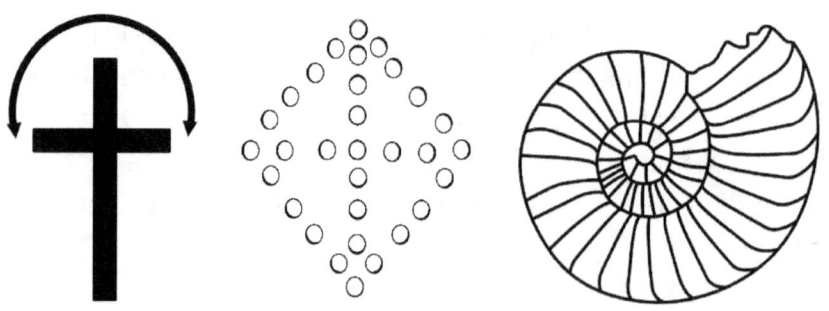

I learned that according to art historian Robert Farris Thomas this Creolized Kongo cosmogram could be "Coded as a cross, a quartered circle or diamond, a seashell spiral, or a special cross with solar emblems at each ending - the sign of the four moments of the sun is the Kongo emblem of spiritual continuity and renaissance par excellence."

In Thompson's Flash of the Spirit: African & Afro-American Art & Philosophy and Face of the Gods: Art and Altars of Africa and the African Americas, I learned that unbeknownst to most, we, African Americans, did not lose our culture. Remnants of our ancestral African past such as our art, food, music, dance to religious expression, etc., survived. As I thought about this, I recalled seeing Kongo imagery and diamond shape emblems all throughout my grandparents, great-grandparents and great aunts and uncles' home. When I asked my mom and other elders in my family why certain practices were done and they could not give me an answer. It became apparent to me what African Americans lost was the philosophy and theology behind our cultural practice.

It was upon making this realization I happened to be looking at my grandmother's obituary where it read in place of her birth date and death date, "Sunrise" and "Sunset."

It was at that moment, something told me, "This (the Sunrise and Sunset) is the Kemetic Ra."

Quickly, I looked up the *Story of Ra and Oset* and that is when I found the key to understanding Kemetic spirituality and an adequate substitute to fill the philosophical and theological void created by slavery.

The Maa Aankh

In the *Story of Ra and Oset*, Oset devises a plan to trick Ra into revealing his Secret Name by creating a serpent that inflicted the great king with illness. Ra stated that although he was the creator of everything, he could not cure himself of the illness. He called all of his children (creation) and called upon them to drive the illness out of him but none could cure their king. Finally, Oset appeared and told Ra that she could cure him but to do so, she needed his Secret Name.

Initially, Ra refused to reveal his Secret Name to her stating at one point, *"I am Khepera in the morning, I am Ra at noon, and I am Tmu at evening."* But, Oset told Ra that the poison continues to persist because he had no revealed his name. Finally, after much deliberation, Ra took Oset aside and revealed his name to her. After doing so, Oset kept her promise and cure poison.

Who or what is Ra?

Contrary to archeologists and historians' belief, Ra is not the sun-god or the sun, which in the Kemetic language is called aten (like atom, coincidence or not?). The sun was used to symbolize Ra, which symbolizes the Power of God.

What was Ra's Secret Name?

The Story appears to end without revealing his name but Ra's name was "Hidden". Hidden in the Kemetic language is "Amen" or "Amun," which is the same term that appears at the end of most prayers. Ra's Secret Name is Amun Ra, the Hidden Ra.

Inspired by the Kongo Cross and using Kemetic philosophy, led me to find that Amun Ra corresponds to the midnight moon.

In other words, Amun Ra is the Hidden or Secret Power of God, which per the Kongo Cross is also the source of rebirth. This discovery led me to find the maa aankh cosmogram.

The maa aankh is composed of the Kemetic terms maa meaning "balance, law, order, truth, etc." and aankh, which means "life, to swear an oath." Hence, maa aankh means the "Order of Life," the "Righteous Living" and/or to "Swear an Oath to Live Truth."

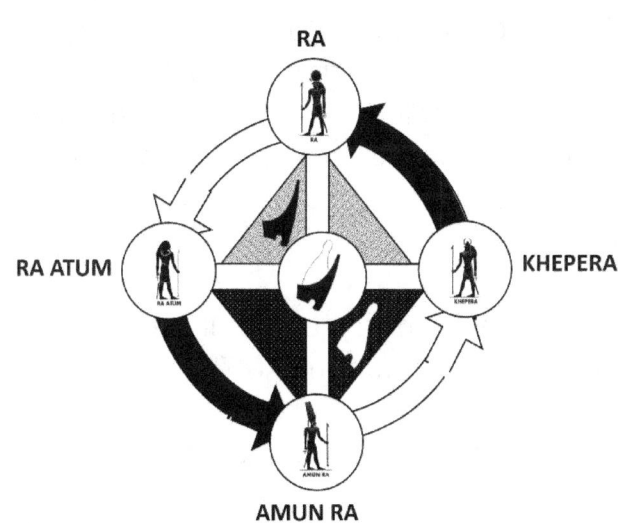
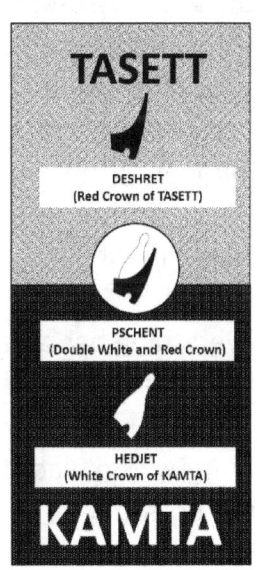

The maa aankh illustrates that there is a horizontal line called nyun, which divides our reality into two lands (realms): TASETT and KAMTA.

TASETT (the Red Lands symbolized by the red Deshret crown), the

top half of the maa aankh, represents the physical realm or the realm we perceive with our five senses – that is what we can smell, taste, see, hear and touch. Consequently, we believe that the only things that exist are real. In fact, TASETT convinces us that accidents, coincidences, mistakes and other chaotic random events are the norm. When in truth nothing occurs without due cause. Plants do not grow overnight. Babies are not born and in a matter of hours become adults. People do not suddenly fall and

become ill. We do not suddenly become impoverished. No one suddenly just changes their mind. Everything that physically exists has an initial Cause but due to the concept of time. We lack the inability to see the whole of reality, which leads us to make the gross assumption that the only things we see – hear, smell, taste and touch (in the physical realm) is real. In other words, the TASETT is the realm of illusions. It is referred to as a desert because deserts are empty, void of life, void of power and full of mirages. When in actuality, the physical realm is fraction of the whole overall reality. It represents a fraction or 10 percent of the whole reality.

Everything has a Cause or a Beginning (regardless if we understand it or not) and it can be found in KAMTA.

KAMTA (the Black Lands symbolized by the white Hedjet crown), the bottom half of the maa aankh, represents the spiritual realm or the realm we perceive with our intuition. KAMTA is the realm of solutions. We connect to this realm every time we get brilliant and creative ideas. It what Swiss psychiatrist Carl G. Jung called the collective unconsciousness. It is what good and strong mothers call "mother wit" or the source of "mother's intuition." Successful entrepreneurs and sharp business people usually refer to this realm and tell others to follow their "gut instinct." While spiritual people have been known to call it throughout the ages the "sixth sense." KAMTA represents the majority or 90 percent of reality.

Although, the horizontal nyun line divides KAMTA (the spiritual realm) and TASETT (the physical realm). The horizontal nyun line create a veil, which erases our memory prior to us being physically born. Thus, when we are physically born, we all pass through it and forget that we are souls with past lives, and we forget why we are here.

However, it is the vertical Maa line that mirrors what exists above, below and vice versa. In other words, the Maa line reveals that nature is highly complex and that the only thing that is predictable about nature, is that it is unpredictable. It is because of the Maa, we know that a sum of small pulses creates a host of cosmic events. Maa is Balance, Law, Truth and Order. Things that appear to be created at random like snowflakes, scientists have found have an order because reveals that small changes now, can have large effects later. In other words, every little thought you had in your life, propelled you to this point today.

Since there is no other being on the planet that is unique like the human being. People identified their soul with the sun because the human soul like the sun, rises at daybreak, peaks at midday, sets at sunset, and is mysteriously reborn at midnight. These four moments of the sun symbolized by the four disks at each end of maa aankh are called Khepera (the Creative Ra/sunrise), Ra (the Visible Ra/midday), Ra Atum (the Complete Ra/sunset) and Amun Ra (the Hidden Ra/midnight). Together they reveal the path of reincarnation and the process of spiritual rebirth.

KHEPERA: The "Coming into existence (RA)" is symbolized by the scarab beetle because the scarab beetles lay their eggs in dung, which symbolizes nothing or no-form. Then scarabs roll the dung balls that have their eggs embedded in them into holes.

KHEPERA

After which, the dung balls are buried and the larvae would be born. The Kemetians saw this as a sign of birth, resurrection and renewal from nothing, hence creation similar to how a potter gives form to a lump of clay (no-thing).

Since everything in nature seems to awaken at sunrise and take form signifying the awakening of consciousness.

This moment is called Khepera (the Creative Ra). Khepera is all of the creative forces of the Supreme Being and is symbolized by the rising sun, lower life, plants, eggs, newborns, children (pre-adolescent), etc. The color associated with this moment is black and it is called in KiKongo Kala.

RA: After everything in nature has awaken from its' slumber, the world is full of activity especially around midday. This moment is called Ra and is symbolized by the peregrine falcons. Peregrine falcons are unique birds of prey that hunt medium sized birds usually from dawn to dusk, or nocturnally when necessary. When diving from above during a hunt, falcons on the average can reach speeds 200 miles per hour and live approximately 67 years of age. Understanding how these animals behave it is easy to see why the Kemetic people symbolized Ra as a falcon.

Ra is the "Living Ra" or the "Visible Ra" symbolizing diurnal activity. Ra was usually depicted as a youthful man with a falcon head but was also seen as an elderly and cruel ruler. This is the reason the term Ra also means "ruler" the hovering of the falcon was seen as a physical manifestation of the midday sun. All

activity that corresponds to the day fell under Ra's dominion. For instance, since falcons hunted from dawn to dusk. The Kemetians called this aggressive energy Ra or epitome of masculinity, Hru Aakhuti, the Hru of the Horizon. Hru Aakhuti is the Kemetic divinity of iron and patrons of warriors because he symbolizes hard work from beginning to end.

The pinnacle of the maa aankh not only symbolizes Ra (the midday sun) but, the northern direction, maleness, the peak of physical strength, logic and rational thinking symbolized by the Right Eye of Ra (the left-hemisphere of the brain). The color of this moment is red and is called in KiKongo Tukula.

Aakhut: The Right Eye of RA
(Solar Eye)

RA ATUM

RA ATUM (**Tum** or **Atum** *RA*): Once the sun begins to set, the activity around the world seems to slow down as evening nears. This moment is symbolized as a mature man indicating that he is fulfilled. Ra Atum signifies the end of harvest. Therefore, as Ra Atum names indicates, this is the "Complete Ra."

RA Atum is usually portrayed as an old man wearing the double crown of Kemet indicating the beginning of the end. Other times he was just depicted as an elderly man.

It appears that the whole idea of elders being respected stems from the concept of the setting sun because elders seen as individuals who had work from sun up to sun down. The righteous elder became upright individuals, which is why they are alive.

Because of their righteous living, they are like setting suns, preparing to return to the great unknown because they are coming closer to having fulfilled their purpose. The great unknown is ancient times was the land of the ancestors or heaven. Elders were seen as the physical manifestation of the setting sun, while babies were the physical manifestation of the rising sun. Elders were loved and cherished because their wisdom improved the quality of life. Therefore, when death takes an elder, it was seen as death robbing the living of an elder's wisdom. This was seen as a strong pillar being taken from

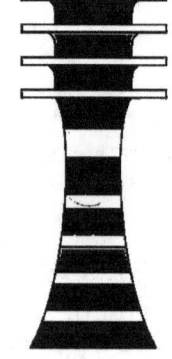

the community. This is how the association between the djet (shown on the left) and backbones were made because both symbolized upright characters. RA Atum symbolizes the transformative powers of the Divine's Power to make one stronger and wiser spiritually (especially after a tests, trials and tribulations). The color associated with this moment is white and it is called in KiKongo Luvemba.

AMUN RA: When the sun sets, from a metaphorical perspective it  disappears but the moon glows in the night sky in the sun's absence. No one knows why we must sleep but we know what happens when we are deprived of sleep. This moment is called Amun Ra because it signifies the mysterious phenomenon that occurs in nature that we have yet to comprehend such as the cycle of rebirth or reincarnation. This moment is also symbolized as the peak of midnight.

 In pre-dynastic Kemet, Amun Ra was symbolized by male sheep or rams because the twisting of the ram's horn symbolized both fertility and rebirth. However, the proverbial "black sheep" phrase seems to

55

stem from the fact that most sheep naturally produce a white fleece. Occasionally, a sheep produces a black fleece, hence the phrase "black sheep" indicating that they are rare. Since one ram can impregnate several sheep, the ram was chosen to symbolize the idea that from "one comes many."

As a symbol of fertility and rebirth, Amun Ra symbolizes the Divine's mysterious power to revitalize, rejuvenate, purify, reform, renew and revive. Consequently, when the Hyksos were expelled from Kemet, the Kemetians credited their victory to Amun Ra, which marked the rebirth of the Kemetic Empire. Amun Ra is therefore symbolized as a man wearing a crown of plumes, usually either sitting or standing to indicate that one has successfully won the war.

Similarly, the polar-opposite of the Ra moment is the Amun Ra moment, which symbolizes the midnight moon, the southern direction, femaleness, femininity, the southern direction, the peak of spiritual strength, abstract, intuitive thinking symbolized by the Left Eye of Ra (the right-hemisphere of the brain). The color associated with this moment is yellow and this moment is called in KiKongo Musoni.

AMUN RA

A thorough thoroughly studying the maa aankh that I discovered that most problems arise in our life around the **Ra moment** because we have acquired impurities from TASETT that are affecting our Ab soul. Consequently, we become egocentric, selfish, fearful, lazy, etc., which results in our ultimate downfall or setting sun (Ra Atum). In order to purify ourselves, our Ab soul has to be reborn (Amun Ra) by passing through the mysterious land of KAMTA.

The interesting thing about the maa aankh is that when I first begin getting interested in Kemetic spirituality, years before I became ill. I had had a vision of it after coming across a chart that showed the different influences that occurred on the planet. I remember I began connecting pieces back then, which

Aabit: The Left Eye of RA
(Lunar Eye)

helped me to see how the spirits (ancestors, spirit guides and the guardian spirits) improve our life, but my so-called spiritual teacher who was supposed to be providing me with guidance discouraged me from following suit, so I abandoned my efforts. Today I see her as a blessing and a lesson for two reasons: First, my experience with her taught me to never to follow anyone blindly. After discovering the maa aankh, I could see the netcharu (guardian spirits) that corresponded to the planets, which were associated with specific hours of the day and times of the year. This mean that a certain of the day and year is under the influence of a particular aspect of the Four Ras (Amun Ra, Khepera, Ra and Ra Atum).

The second reason I consider my "spiritual teacher" a blessing and a lesson is because through her misguided efforts, I met my Npu. I began to see by studying the patterns that occurred in my life that Npu was always around. It was because of Npu, I met Papa, who was a high priest and child of the Yoruba Npu Ellegua. I was beginning to believe that it was Npu who tried to help me to discover the maa aankh years ago. I just did not trust my intuition but my Npu found another way to connect and it was through Papa.

I interpreted this entire experience as a sign that I had been called and I am living proof of someone who almost lost their anointing because of misinformation. This is why, I like many people had read the Kemetic *Story of Osar* but due to the maa aankh, I began using the *story* as a model for my life.

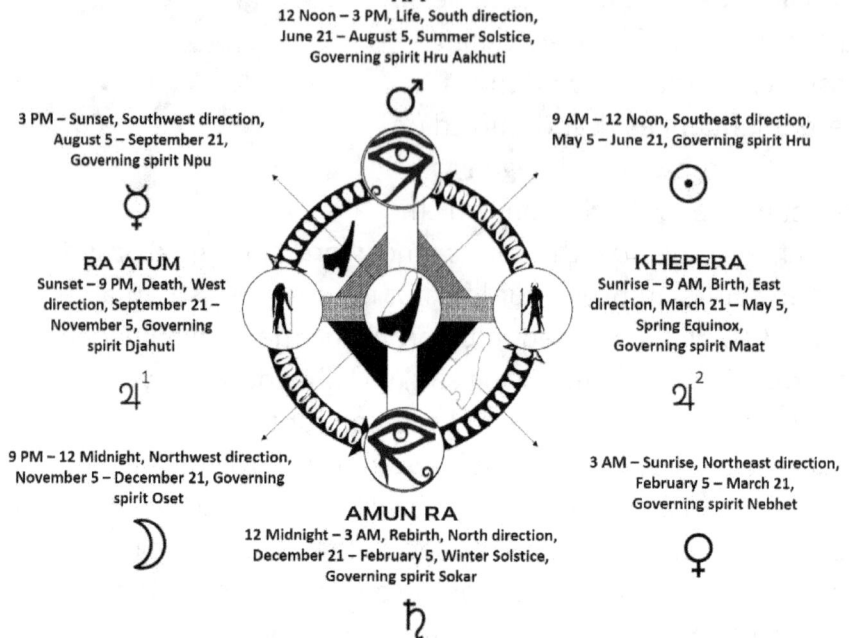

It was not long afterwards that like the Kemetic hero Hru (Horus). I realized that we come or incarnate into TASETT (the world of the living) incomplete so that can go through KAMTA (the world of the dead) in order to become maa kheru (true of voice), which means "born again", complete, mastered and whole, symbolized as Hru and the wearer of the double white and red Pschent crown.

Therefore, whenever an individual begins to have illnesses, obstacles, problems, setbacks, trials, tribulations, troubles, etc., symbolized on the maa aankh as the setting sun (from Ra to Ra Atum). These are signs that one's soul has acquired a host of gross impurities (arrogance, selfishness, vanity, etc.) as result of living in TASETT (the physical realm). Said another way, it can be said that Set has blinded us, in order to purify our soul of the gross impurities we have acquired or have our eye repaired. We must be maa kheru (born again).

Guardian Spirit & Number	Planet	Time of the Day	Time of the Year
Amun Ra Moment			
Sokar, 13 & 17	Saturn $\hbar$	12 AM to 3 AM	Dec. 21–Feb. 5
Nebhet, 5	Venus ♀	3 AM to Sunrise	Feb. 5–Mar. 21
Khepera Moment			
Maat, 2 & 4	Jupiter $♃^2$	Sunrise to 9 AM	Mar. 21–May 5
Hru, 6	Sun ☉	9 AM to 12 PM	May 5–June 21
Ra Moment			
Hru Aakhuti, 3, 4, 7 and 11	Mars ♂	12 PM to 3 PM	June 21–Aug. 5
Npu, 3, 9, 21	Mercury ☿	3 PM to Sunset	Aug. 5–Sep. 21
Ra Atum Moment			
Djahuti, 8	Jupiter $♃^1$	Sunset to 9 PM	Sep. 21–Nov. 5
Oset, 7	Moon ☾	9 PM to 12 AM	Nov. 5–Dec. 21

Lesson Two: Primary Steps for Conducting Rituals

How to Draw the Maa Aankh

Drawing the maa aankh is a ritualized gesture and prayer used to evoke and invoke all of the forces Kemetically. The maa aankh can be drawn anywhere and at any time physically and visually. It can be drawn over people, places and things in order to issue a blessing. It can be drawn on ground, sidewalk, etc. to create het (house/altar for spirits). It can also be drawn in the room of a house or building, and even over the wastepaper baskets to create an artificial crossroad for deployment.

Of course, certain objects like the five spots on dice and places in nature such as crossroads or where city meets forest, etc., naturally have a maa aankh. Other items can have the maa aankh superimposed upon them. For instance, cigars, the open end symbolizes TASETT, while the lit end represents KAMTA. Similar thoughts apply to incense.

Step 1: Draw a horizontal line from left to right, while saying "Nyun." Contemplate on how there is a thin veil that separates the invisible spiritual realm from the visible physical realm.
Step 2: Draw a vertical line from below the horizontal nyun line, while saying "Maa." Contemplate on how Maa mirrors everything that exists within us outside of us, hence "as above so below, as within so without."

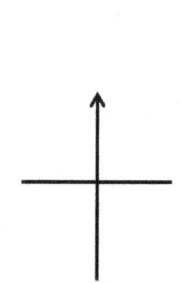

Step 3: Draw a diagonal line from the bottom of the vertical Maa to the right of the horizontal nyun line, while saying "Shu." Contemplate on the original Cause, masculinity, active, logic, enlightenment, sun, light, creation, dominance, upward movement, hot, strong, expansion, hard, movement, etc.

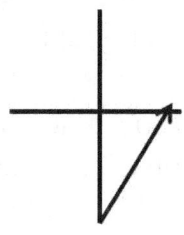

Step 4: From the right side of the horizontal arm, draw a diagonal line to the top of the vertical line, while saying "Tefnut." Contemplate on the original Effect, femininity, passive, intuition, delusion, moon, darkness, cold, submission, contracting, downward movement, night, softness, stillness, etc.

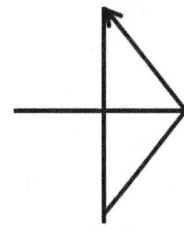

Step 5: Draw a diagonal line from the top of the vertical Maa line to the left arm of the horizontal nyun line, while saying "Shu." Contemplate on how for every action there a reaction is.

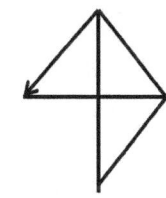

Step 6: Draw a diagonal line from the left arm of the horizontal nyun line to the bottom of the vertical Maa line, while saying "Tefnut." Contemplate on how for every action there a reaction is.

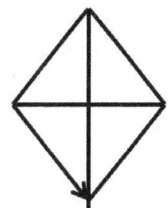

Step 7: Draw a circle counter clockwise circle beginning from the bottom of the vertical Maa line and connecting all of the points. As you do this say the following, "Es Khepera, Ra, Ra Atum Amun." This is a salutation to the Supreme Being Nebertcher that means "Greetings/Hail to the One that Governs Birth, Life, Death and Rebirth."

Contemplate on the four moments of the sun – sunrise, midday, sunset and midnight; and the evolution of the soul – birth, life, death and rebirth.

How to Anoint & Bless Objects Using the Maa Aankh

Any object such as a glass of water, oils, herbs, incense, minerals (e.g. salt), candles, food, homes, etc., can be made sacred (anointed or blessed) by tracing the maa aankh over it. For instance, if you wanted to make your own blessed oil, you would:

1. Place both open palms over the container and imbue it with your power.
2. Speak over the oil by saying that the oil is to be used for anointing, blessing and removing negative influences.
3. Using your right hand, dab extra virgin olive oil, essential oil, conditioned oil, etc. on your index and middle finger.
4. Then trace the maa aankh over the container, while reciting the accompanying evocation.
5. Conclude the blessing by saying, "Thank you."

The above blessing can be used for consecrating herbs, water, etc. Note, that if you feel comfortable, you can also read aloud any of the Psalms of your choosing and include or substitute it in for Step 3. Shamans are not boggled down by dogma. We focus on what works and produces a tangible result.

Finding Your Maa Aankh

Usually when people hear my story, they comment on how they do not want to undergo similar experiences that I have had. I always tell people two things: First, that despite it all, I am glad that I had the experience and I have no regret because of everything that I learned, and. Second, my spirits tried to help me and intervene on numerous occasions but I did not follow because I was not looking at the signs. Not only that, it was because of my spirits I made it out and I am alive today.

The purpose of this exercise is to find your own pattern of events, your maa aankh. Your spirits have been trying to show you a pattern and if you take the time to note significant changes in your life. You will easily see who governing certain areas of your life and who should not be in the picture at all.

For instance, I was born in March, which is the third month of the year. The numbers 3 and 9, which are Npu's numbers are recurring numbers that appear in my life. I met Papa around August, which per the maa aankh is Npu's time of the year.

There are other significant events that I have found when I sat down and reviewed various events. For instance, as I mentioned, I was born around in March, which according to the maa aankh is Nebhet's time of the year. This happens to be the time of the year I receive a lot of money as well. The people I have had the most trouble with are those born during the Amun Ra moment and the Khepera moments. This means these people who make me reflect the most on my behavior.

For the record, this is not an exact science. This is something I discovered after noticing certain patterns that occur in my life. Observing these patterns helped me to identify my spirits and also recognize intrusive spirits that enter into my life.

Write down important date such as your birthday, anniversaries, graduations, etc. as best you can remember. Note significant events that have changed your life.

For a larger view of the maa aankh see the appendix.

THREE:
Acknowledging the Call

According to the maa aankh cosmogram, the Maa makes TASETT a reflection of KAMTA, and vice versa. This means that the spiritual realm is similar to the physical realm in the sense that there are people, who have organized into groups based upon what they have mastered in life. This has been going on for thousands upon thousands of years, which basically has created an organized structured that is governed by the first ancestral spirits to master this particular energy. The first ancestors are called the netcharu.

One can imagine the netcharu as being like a chief of all of these spirits, or a supervisor of millions of worker spirits. This means if we were to envision KAMTA in contemporary times it is like a megacity where each netchar governs a particular building or structure.

If you think of how a multi-billion-dollar business functions, there are low-entry employees, departments that focus on certain parts of the business (e.g. customer service, maintenance, sales, etc.) and various floors dedicated to certain projects, etc. Some business even has sub-departments and there are also special project groups, etc.

Anyone who has ever worked for a business knows that unless you know someone in the higher offices, the only way to be promoted is to prove your self-worth to the company. If a particular higher-up takes interest in you because they see your commitment and you show signs of your dedication to the company. They will work to help you to get your foot in the door, so that you can advance to the next level. And so, it continues this way until you get to the top.

Well, the same applies somewhat in the spiritual realm with the difference being that prove your self-worth based upon what you have mastered in life. In other words, you advance based upon what you have mastered or know. The things are that since there are no physical boundaries in the spiritual realm, the higher level is composed of spirits who have demonstrated more self-mastery. Higher level spirits similar to higher-ups can help lower spirits ascend to higher levels but it is only if the lower spirit demonstrates commitment by being willing to assist their loved ones in the physical realm. This is because a spirit's evolution is linked their descendant's growth in the physical realm. Typically, if a person is prosperous in life, it is because their ancestral spirits are prosperous in death. However, if the person is suffering in life, it is because their ancestors are suffering in death.

In other words, the problems that we have in our life are problems that our ancestors have in the hereafter. For instance, if you are trying to improve or increase your finances but every time you try. Something happens and you end up having another financial setback. It is because your ancestors had problems as well with their finances when they were alive and are stuck dealing with this same problem in the hereafter. This is what the ancients called Hell.

Therefore, every time we are stuck dealing with a problem. It is imagined that there is an aakhu that is struggling with this same issue in the KAMTA. The remedy is to venerate and make offerings to your ancestors, so that they can use the essence of these things, to assist them in reaching higher levels within the hereafter. In return for offerings received, the ancestors will send messages to their descendants in the forms of visions, dreams, prophecies, etc. that will improve their life.

Therefore, the first step to spiritual growth is to acknowledge that you have been called. This signals to your spirits that you recognize them and are willing to work with them to achieve common goals. For instance, none of what I discovered or learned would have been realized had I not began honoring my ancestors and made the connection between Ra and my grandmother's obituary. I initially honored my ancestors by mimicking various traditions because I did not know any better.

Since I was raised in an Apostolic Pentecostal household, I did not really understand the purpose of venerating my ancestors. The church never really explained or clarified a lot of concepts, so I had to learn what ancestors were and why they exist. It was through my experience with them that I began to recognize certain characteristics of how spirits manifested themselves in my life.

What are Spirits?

Spiritual forces or spirits are the basically the surviving consciousness of people who died in a reasonable manner. Spirits are thinking and rational entities that are capable of existing without a physical body. In other words, spirits are basically another word for energy. To distinguish between benevolent spirits and malevolent spirits, people in the Middle Ages began calling benevolent spirits that assist and clear energy, angels. Then, they called malevolent spirits that block, hinder and obstruct energy, demons (in the Judeo-Christian tradition). All spirits are minor emanations of our Perfect Creator, the Supreme Being, who is called in Kemet Nebertcher—the Lord of All Things.

Why Do Spirits Exist?

The one thing that people need to understand about our Perfect Creator is that Nebertcher is an infinitely wise and intelligent Supreme Spirt. As with people, when our Perfect Creator is called upon unexpectedly, our Perfect Creator may be busy doing something else in our universe or some other universe. Therefore, the Supreme Being created minor spirits to assist when the Divine is busy, by taking it upon themselves to render help when our Perfect Creator is called upon. This is the only way our Perfect Creator can address all of the petitions and requests that come to the Divine from all over the world.

There are a countless number of spirits but there are a select few who assist us in our life. Since Nebertcher – Our Perfect Creator – gives us the freedom to choose the life we are going to live. We each have helping spirits, guardian spirits and foe spirits.

How did this happen? Well very briefly (because this story will be covered in detailed in the near future), according to the Kemetic tradition, there were two brothers named Osar and Set who were given the power to rule over Kemet in pre-dynastic times. During this time, the Kemetic people were in a constant state of war with one another. Until the eldest brother Osar began teaching people about the Maa. In a relatively short time, Osar had a massive following and was able to unify the people of pre-Kemet peacefully. This angered his youngest brother Set, who out of jealousy plotted against Osar, killed him and usurped his throne. Thanks to Osar's loving and devoted wife, Oset, who gave birth to Osar's heir, Hru. Set was challenged and eventually the throne of Osar was reclaimed through Osar interceding on his son's behalf.

Consequently, Osar was recognized as being the first enlightened and honored ancestor and became the first guardian spirit or netchar, hence his title the *Lord of the Underworld*. The Underworld is not hell as filmmakers depict but a code referring to our deep mind, the Superconscious or BA. Therefore, Osar corresponds to our Superconscious, Higher Self or BA, and all benevolent spirits or helping spirits are aligned with him.

What are Helping Spirits?

Our Osar, who is our primary guardian spirit, is accompanied by benevolent spirits or so-called good spirits (good angels), which are deceased people who after seeing their life flash before their eyes, and realizing how they could have done things differently. Choose to correct their mistakes by offering constructive advice, empowering suggestions, assistance, blessings, healing and protection. Basically, these are the souls of people who exist as a spirit now, that agree to assist us in becoming the creators of our own destinies and masters of our own fate. It is similar to an elder instructing a child on the mistakes they made in life, so that the child will avoid certain pitfalls. Many of these spirits are our deceased blood relatives but not all of them, which is why they are called helping spirits or aakhu.

Aakhu in the Kemetic language means stars. Stars were used by ancient people to help them to navigate through the world. Therefore, aakhu are basically helping spirit or guides and although most people refer to these spirits as angels. Technically speaking the aakhu are our ancestors and spirit guides. The title aakhu is used to describe ancestral spirits and spirit guides because they were seen as people who had a positive and inspiring influence on our sahu (subconscious) while alive and continue to inspire us after their physical death. Aakhu are all focused on evolution, spiritual development, etc. of a family, community, group, society, nation and even the world, and this is the difference between benevolent spirits and malevolent spirits.

Aakhu are our greatest spiritual allies because they provide us with courage, protection and vision into the great unknown. They offer us insight about their lives, which can aid and ease us of some of the setbacks we will encounter due to the human experience. In other words, they provide us with the map we need whenever we feel lost. Remember, they lived on Earth before, so they know of the hardships that we have to face. By assisting us they help us to advance, but through us they also are able to spiritually grow as well.

When you work with the aakhu, you offer them spiritual energy in the form of offerings and prayers, so that they can return this energy back to us in the form of spiritual assistance, spiritual development, enlightenment and personal empowerment. They can also be called upon for assistance in spiritual healing, spiritual cleansings and spiritual blessings.

Our Osar picks and chooses who our aakhu will be. As a result, all of our aakhu will have a varying level of consciousness. Some of these spirits may have been chosen by our primary aakhu because they mastered a particular lesson in life. Other spirits may have been chosen because they are knowledgeable of the task that we have to accomplish. Some may have been chosen because they need to learn a lesson in order for them to ascend to the next level. Whatever the case, our primary aakhu selects these spirits to assist us at a particular point in our life because they can tune in and help us with our purpose.

What are Foe Spirits?

Our world is about balance and just like we have benevolent helping spirits, we also have negative spirits. Our primary foe spirit is Osar's youngest brother Set, so just like Osar is accompanied by the benevolent aakhu who are helping spirits that are associated with our deep mind, the Superconscious, Higher Self or BA. Set, because of his envious, violent, chaotic, etc. actions and behaviors became immortalized as the primary foe spirit, who corresponds to our lower self, subconscious or sahu with malevolent spirits.

Most people call malevolent or foe spirits demons but they are spirits who have chosen to stay in the same rut. Many times, (not always) foe spirits have died violently or through suicide. Most foe spirits are chaotic, confused and misguided like psychotic human beings. They offer no constructive advice or suggestions that could improve the life of the living. Instead they encourage the living to follow the same unwise destructive path that they followed when alive. For instance, if these spirits when alive were involved in criminal activities. They will continue to inspire others to take the same path that they took, knowing it leads to nowhere.

Contrary to popular belief, just because these spirits are evil does not mean they will remain evil. These spirits at any time can choose to change, which is the reason our Perfect Creator puts our fate in our hands. All they have to do is choose to do what is right versus what is easy, which will cause their soul to advance. It is a long and tedious process since spirits do not have a physical body, which is the reason all spirits (good and bad) choose instead to reincarnate back to the earth.

Like the benevolent aakhu spirits, foe spirits are the spirits of people who once walked the earth but did not aspire to anything. Contrary to the horror film industry, these spirits are not evil per se. They are simply confused, misguided people in life who were up-to-no-good that became the same confused, misguided and up-to-no-good entities in death. This is not to say that there are no evil spirits but in general most negative or impure spirits are not evil. For this reason, these spirits are called aapepu, which is the Kemetic word for parasitic snakes and worms.

In Kemetic lore, the aapep were known for killing Ra or draining the life-force out of living beings. In the Book of Overthrowing the Aapep, the aapep were killed, hacked into pieces, dismembered and thrown into the void, but they always managed to come back because they are negative spirits. So, in ancient times the Kemetic people make images of the aapep out of wax or drawing. Then, they would spit and mutilate the image while chanting victory over the aapep and burning the images.

As I mentioned, I was never taught about spirits in the church. In the church spirits were either classified as being of God or of the devil. What I found to be very interesting was that a lot of times people would get slain in the spirit, shout, speak-in-tongues, and soon as the Holy Ghost left them. They would return to their devilish ways. Understanding that demons are really confused and misguided souls of the dead. Explains why these people were able to speak-in-tongues is because they became possessed by the aapepu, which is the reason back-in-the-day, before preaching, stepping on to the pulpit, seeking a vision or doing any godly work, people would pray and fast.

Aapepu as far as I can tell and from observing how they functioned in my family are the souls of people who are considered outcast. For instance, in my family there were certain members of my extended family who were excluded from family functions because of their lifestyle. It was not that they were not loved or welcomed but these family members compared to the rest of my extended family were into "alternative" lifestyles. And, a lot of their choices resulted in them having a lot of bad luck, drama, accidents, all sorts of freakish tragedies, and issues with the law. The reason the Kemetic people called them parasitic worms and noxious serpents because they have a negative or uninspiring effect on our sahu (subconscious). Similar to how a parasite or snakes would wander into your home and disrupt the natural harmony of things, negative spirits do the same thing.

When negative spirits try to enter our physical bodies, they use parasites as a medium and some of them are responsible for making our egotistical behaviors. Contrary to popular belief, the aapepu (negative, malevolent, confused, misguided, trickster, ghostlike spirits) do not haunt good people because they want to make trouble in their life. Aapepu are attracted to us because of the thoughts and ideas that we hold in our mind. When we focus on low thoughts and ideas, we attract these negative spirits to us.

The horror film industry makes it seem as if people are just vulnerable to negative spirits because it is easier to make money peddling fear. Most aapepu are like loud obnoxious people that you have to ignore while riding on the bus, the train, etc. However, since negative spirits or aapepu are confused, misguided, chaotic and ignorant spirits that egotistically focus on their survival. They are low ancestral spirits associated with Set (animalistic, egotistical, selfish, etc.) behaviors. Just like Set was ousted, these spirits when they were alive were not welcomed and in death are not welcomed either unless they change their ways. If you are meant to learn a lesson, then you must learn that lesson in order to advance to the next level. Hence the saying, "there is no escaping your destiny."

Therefore, learning self-control can make aapepu gain self-control. If you struggle with an issue, it really an issue against the aapepu. For instance, if you struggle with alcohol you are fighting one of your lower spirits. By learning self-control, you teach the spirit control, which is the lesson to be learned from aapepu.

How Do You Know You Are Being Guided by Benevolent Spirits?

When we follow benevolent spirits they usually speak through the intuition of our BA and discourage us from following our ego. Our primary aakhu makes connections and uses his influence to intercede on our behalf. Similar to how Osar interceded on Hru's behalf, our primary aakhu acts as lawyers by searching for the best deals that will encourage spiritual growth.

Whenever we are experiencing hardships, having problems, experiencing any type of setback, etc. We can always reach out to our primary aakhu who will connect us to our aakhu (ancestral spirits and spirit guides). Together they will influence situations that lead us away from accidents and disturbances; bump into you thus causing you to miss being hit by a vehicle; cause you to be in the right place at the right time for opportunities to fall into our lap; or give us the inspiration we need to complete a project that will result in us being prosperous.

How Do You Know You Are Being Blinded by Foe Spirits?

When we follow our Set who speaks through our sahu (lower self, subconscious), every egocentric impulse, every negative action and behavior, every malicious word, every vicious action. Every time we act out of anger, guilt, shame, fear and jealousy. Every time we are scornful, disrespectful, nasty, vindictive, malicious and spiteful. Every time we swindle, deceive, cheat, etc. Our Set attracts negative spirits called aapepu to create chaos, havoc and destruction.

Together Set with the aapepu cause miscommunication between people in order to break-up relationships. They hide keys and other things of importance. They cover your eyes and create blind spots, causing you to miss the car in the other lane and have an accident. They confuse messages resulting in arguments and fights and other mishaps.

Simply put, every time we give into reactive emotions like fear, jealousy, selfishness, egotism, etc. like Set (foe spirit), we attract the negatives spirits or aapepu to our sides. However, when we are proactive by being level-headed, cool, patient, etc. like Osar (primary aakhu), we attract the positive spirits or aakhu to us.

Why Do We Need Helping Spirit?

According to the maa aankh cosmogram, when we are born, we all pass through the veil of nyun at the Khepera moment (when we are born). Most of our memories of our past lives, our true godlike nature and the reason we are here is erased. Just in case you are wondering why our memories are erased prior to our arrival, it is because if we knew about our divine nature, knew who we were and knew our purpose. We would know the future and we would not be able to achieve our goal of achieving fulfilment. For instance, if you knew that there is a possibility that you may break your leg by learning how to ride a bike, would you still try to learn this skill? Most people would not because most people try to avoid falling at all cost without understanding. That the purpose of falling is so that you know how to stand back up.

So, since we (the living) do not remember our purpose, our helping spirits who are still on the other side of the nyun line, can assist us because they can see and remembering everything. As a result, these spirits will help us to achieve goals that our in alignment with our true purpose. They accomplish this by communicating to us intuitively. Because our helping spirits have been selected by our primary aakhu and they reside in KAMTA, they have the tendency to send us flashes of intuitive insight. Flashes correspond to the whiteness of Osar's hedjet crown. Many times, these thoughts that appear to come out of nowhere provide helpful clues on what we should do. A lot of time, these thoughts that sound like voices in our head such as, "Slow down!" "She is cheating on you", and so on are ignored because we may not like what is being said. But our helping spirits are not here to sugarcoat life but to help us achieve our purpose. When messages are received, it is best to pick up on the clues and surrender.

Obviously, the reason the aapepu cannot help us is because they are on the same side of the nyun with us and therefore have a limited perspective. This is the reason; we are not fascinated by ghosts because they cannot assist us in our growth and development. We work with the aakhu because they can provide us with the insight, we need to improve the quality of life.

How do Spirits Communicate to Us?

There are several ways that spirits will try to communicate with us and below are some of the most common ways:

- Animals: All of the netcharu have totem animals that are associated with them and the spirits that walk with them will use them to communicate messages to you. If you are performing a ritual and you see one of these animals. It is confirmation that they got the message and are on the job. If you are not doing a ritual and you see one of the netchar's animals. You need to pay attention to your thoughts and/or how you feel immediately after seeing it.

- Celaje (pronounced say-la-hay): Celaje in Spanish is said to be small clouds or colored clouds, but spiritually speaking. It refers to the shadows that we see out of the corners of your eye. In Cuba and Puerto Rico, it is usually interpreted as an auspicious sign that your spirits are near you.

- Dreams: One of the most common ways spirits communicate to us is through our dreams because we are in a relaxed state of mind. Remember, our BA cannot give us creative ideas when we are tensed, stressed and wired up. So, many spirits will visit us when we are sleep and give us messages. When you receive messages in your dreams, the key to interpreting them is to review how it makes you feel. For instance, a recurring theme that appears in my dreams, is me being chased by zombies. Zombies are my spirits' way of reminding me old and useless habits.

  I have also found that spirits will also send your messages as visions while taking showers, washing dishes or performing some other mindless tasks.

- Hearing Your Name: Hearing your name called and no one is around is an old belief that spirits are around. One common belief is that when you hear your name called it is a negative spirit that is trying to misguide you like the legendary Greek Sirens.

The old folk belief of whistling in the house or when no one is around is based upon the belief that you are trying to get a spirit's attention. For that matter, any spirit (benevolent or malevolent) is liable to answer.

- Insects: I have found that some ancestral spirits will use insects. For instance, when my wife's mom passed away several months later, we kept seeing her favorite insect – ladybugs. Now, seeing one or two ladybugs can be considered a coincidence but more than three is definitely a sign. I mean, I kept seeing different color ladybugs in my office, car and in my house, which was a clear sign that it was definitely her. Some other insects that spirits seem to be fond of communicating with are butterflies and dragonflies.

- Music: Often when we hear music that reminds us of someone who passed. This is a sign that a spirit is trying to communicate with us. Sometimes spirits will keep playing a song in your mind continuously called an "earworms." Other times, you may just turn on the radio or hear music from a passing vehicle. If any of these songs reminds you of someone who is passed. It is important that you pay attention to the lyrics and/or how the song makes you feel.

- Moving Objects: Chill out! I am not talking about actual objects floating in the air as they do in horror films. No. Spirits do have a habit of moving things. If you get an urge to move something because it seems or feels better. This is most likely inspiration from a spirit. For instance, I remember when my grandfather passed away. I felt like he wanted his photo on my Npu altar, so I placed his photo there. After a month or so, he wanted to be moved to my ancestral altar (het aakhu), which is where he has been ever since. As far as I can tell, my grandfather did not know anything about Npu. He was a Freemason but as far as I can figure. He wanted to be moved to Npu's het because Npu is a crossroad and gateway spirit that leads the dead to their new role.

Negative spirits move things as well. Remember, Set blinded Hru resulting in him not seeing the obvious. Have you ever laid something down like your keys, money, important papers, etc. somewhere? When you went back you could not find them. Then, later you either find them in the exact location or somewhere you know you did not go? This is the work of Set creating confusion. In some cultures, it is believed to be the spirits of witches.

- Numbers: Have you ever looked at a clock and seems as if it has stopped or you wake-up at a particular time to see a particular time? For instance, sometimes I happen to pass by a room and the clock reads 1:11, which is 1+1+1=3. I usually interpret this as a sign from my Npus since Npu's number is 3, and Hru Aakhuti because his number is 11, thus it is a warning sign informing me to be cautious. Understand, there is no right or wrong way of interpreting numerical signs. It all depends upon how a particular number makes you feel based upon your experience.

It should also be noted that clocks are not the only way spirits communicate with numbers. Spirits will also use numbers in other ways such as appearing on license plates, the number of events, etc.

- Playing with electricity: I have heard of spirits playing with electricity but in my experience. It is usually negative spirits that do this. For instance, they will cause a light bulb to blowout in order to startle you. As far as I can tell, negative spirits get a little energy from doing this. When this occurs, it is a clear sign that you need to cleanse your space.

- Senses are enhanced: Do you feel a light brushing on your hand or arm? Do you smell fragrances or perfumes that remind you of someone who has passed? These are signs that spirits are near you. Other signs involving your physical senses are an intense temporary ringing in your ear, which is believed by many to be a sign that information is being downloaded from your BA into your sahu, hence processing a request.

- Another sign of your sense being enhanced is the famous "Spidey sense." This is where you feel like someone is playing in your hair or your head tingling. These are all signs is also a sign that spirits are present and alerting you to something.

- Synchronicities: Spirits can give us all sorts of signs but sometimes they can cause two or more events to occur that are highly unlikely to occur by chance, in a very meaningful way. For instance, have you ever thought about family member or a friend? Then suddenly, they call or receive a message from them, which has you saying, "I was just thinking about you." Besides revealing that we are connected, this is one-way spirits getting us to see that we are on to something.

- Thoughts: Intellectual spirits have the tendency to share messages to us by appearing as thoughts and ideas in our head. You may get a thought or an idea that reminds you of something a relative did when they were alive. For instance, I was once reminded how during my family reunions as a child. My brothers, cousins and I had to take turn churning the ice cream maker. Hours later, we all were able to enjoy homemade ice cream but the image and thought that popped in my head was a reminder of how we (my family) work together. It was a reminder that we need to continue to do the same in the future.

For the record, I am aware that a lot of this sounds pretty fanciful but we have to remember that the purpose of myths is to help us to reconnect back to the natural world. There are a lot of truths that cannot be explained using hard-cold, scientific fact. The truths in regard to how to connect with each other and maintain balance nature are based upon our Ab soul and cannot be measured except by the spirit. However, the general rule to remember is that you should never blindly trust spirits. Always treat information received from them with a degree of skepticism.

Who Is Considered a Helping Spirit or Aakhu?

Since Osar chooses the aakhu who will assist us in life, as you can imagine there are a lot of aakhu that exist. In previous books, I have mentioned that we all have different types of aakhu. For instance, some of these spirits will inspire us using history, while others will inspire us through religion, etc. Further investigation has led to me discover that these spirits are basically our spiritual DNA.

First it must be understood that we all have ancestry that goes back to the beginning of time, when the first of our ancestors walked the planet. To get technical, we have as many ancestors as we have cells within our body. All of these ancestral spirits contribute to our behavior, how we act, talk, speak, etc. but they do not all play a major role in our life. There is only a handful of aakhu who have been chosen to walk with us in this lifetime. Some of these aakhu have been with us since birth, while others come into our life for a brief moment to get us to move in a specific direction. Some aakhu have a stronger influence on us more so than others do, while we all may share a common aakhu who ties us all together.

Since it is our actions and behaviors that attracts or repels spirits to us. We bump shoulders with many aakhu that are found in places of nature or places of power, like in the woods, forests, crossroads, front and backdoor, etc. and for this reason. These aakhu are closely associated with certain netchar (guardian spirits) like Npu. However other aakhu because of their heroic deeds can be called upon by remembering their unique story, like Harriet Tubman who can still free people as she had done in the Underground Railroad, or Black Hawk the Sauk leader who fought against government oppression.

The aakhu are able to communicate with us whenever we make a soul connection with them. This is how we get a plethora of different aakhu. The following is a list of the most prominent spirits that appear in our life:

Primary Aakhu – are ancestral spirits who speak to us through our BA (Superconscious/Higher Self). These spirits are usually associated with the netchar Osar and accompany us in life from birth. They are responsible for organizing life events and gathering the various aakhu who will assist us in life.

Biological Aakhu – are ancestral spirits who are related to us by blood. These aakhu are usually associated with the netchar Oset and have a strong sense of family. Biological aakhu are typically very concerned with maintaining tradition for the benefit of the family clan. Although, immediate family ancestral spirits are included in this group. Most of these are distant ancestral spirits whom most of us would not remember.

Historical Aakhu – are ancestral spirits that have made contributions that have changed the world such as Frederick Douglas, Harriet Tubman, Malcolm X, Dr. Martin Luther King, etc. Most historical aakhu usually have a street, building, school, etc. named after them. This aakhu is a reflection of the times and will link you with other people with similar backgrounds. For instance, ever noticed that people with similar interest frequent familiar events, groups and movements. They are all united by a common historical aakhu. I have found that these aakhu help us to shape our political views and raise the consciousness of the community. These aakhu are associated with the netchar Hru and usually inspire us through history.

Mythical Aakhu – are spirits who may have been a priest, priestess, shaman, a spiritualist, reader, a witch, monk, nun, some form of asceticism. They were usually involved in some esoteric spiritual system. Most mythical aakhu were syncretized into biblical characters as Moses, King Solomon, etc. These are the spirits help us to make sense out of our life. Have you ever noticed that some people do not seem to have commonsense? It is because these spirits have not been activated or are not properly being motivated to assist in an individual's life. These aakhu typically are associated with the netchart Maat.

Healing Aakhu – these spirit guides basically help us in all forms of healing. If you are fond of alternative forms of healing, it most likely because you are being influenced by this spirit. These aakhu are associated with the netchar Sokar and will give you hints and ideas of herbal remedies, etc. When ill they can be called upon to help you to find a good health practitioner.

Sweetwater Aakhu – are spirits that are typically associated with Nebhet. Many of these spirits are in some shape, fashion and form connected to the rivers and streams. They assist us in building relationships.

Personal Guide Aakhu – are the spirits that most people speak about when they talk about spirit guides. These are the aakhu that intercede just in the nick of time and save us from making disastrous mistakes. These spirit guides are associated with the netchar Npu and they are like your personal scout who goes ahead of you and warns you when the road is clear and safe. They will guide you away from certain dangers and lead you to fortunes.

Warrior Aakhu – are spirits that protect us and keep us safe from harm. These spirits are associated with Hru Aakhuti. They guard and protect us but also teach us the difference between courage and foolhardiness. They give us an air of courage.

Teaching Aakhu – are basically spirit guides from that may or may not be kin who have crossed bloodlines and/or cultural lines to be an inspirational guide. They are usually of a different ethnicity and culture. These spirits are very protective and concerned because we are walking down paths that either they created or have walked themselves. These spirits could have mastered specific skills in their life or just taken an interest in our development and assumed the role as an adoptive parent or godparent. Many teaching aakhu are also responsible for helping one learn divination. These aakhu are typically associated with the netchar Djahuti.

I have found that certain physical sensations seem to correspond to certain aakhu. For instance, ever notice how you give someone advice that you should be following as well, this could be your Teaching aakhu encouraging you not to be a hypocrite. When Primary aakhu (who are associated with Osar) speak, it is common to see ideas, thoughts and symbols appear to you on the right side. Biological aakhu, which are associated with Oset typically send you fond memories of deceased family members when the stomach muscles are relaxed. Historical aakhu, which are associated with Hru will relay messages of courage, honor and respect, while speaking to you through the heart and lungs. Healing aakhu, who are associated with Sokar, will give you ideas encouraging you to be resilient and tend to speak through your bones, which feels as if, they hover over you. Sweet water aakhu, which are associated with Nebhet, are fond of beautiful things and tend to speak through the eyes (and ears) by drawing your gaze to people, places and things that catch your attention. Mystical aakhu, which are associated with Maat, are the spirits that usually inspire us to follow spiritual pursuits. While our Warrior aakhu, which are associated with Hru Aakhuti protect us from danger and steer us away from negative influences.

Although Set is considered a primary foe spirit, technically speaking he is a netchar (guardian spirit) and the aapepu are the spirits associated with him. These spirits tend make our skin crawl, hair stand on our neck, etc. when near. They will also give you the feeling that something is following you. Aapepu have the ability to draw upon all of the negative influences of the aakhu. For instance, aapepu can draw upon Sweet water aakhu and lead you to chase after something that catches your attention that may not be in your best interest.

Please note that this is not an exact science and it is not intended to diagnose. This is simply based upon observations that I have made.

Special African American African Spirits

It should be noted that any of the helper aakhu can be come from different cultures and for this reason they are known as cultural aakhu. Cultural aakhu usually are not related to us but for some reason have agreed to assist us in our growth. For instance, you could have Asian Warrior Aakhu who walks with Hru Aakhuti if you are trying to master the Asian martial arts like karate, tae kwon do, etc. You could have an African Mystical Aakhu who inspires you to purchase an African figurine and place it next to Maat because they want to assist you in divination. It is possible to have a Native American Sweetwater Aakhu that inspires you. However, there are two aakhu that people of African descent in the Americas all have and they are known throughout the Afro-Diaspora as Los Negros, Preto Velhos and La Madama and El Congo. In North America, the female archetype aakhu is known as Momma or Auntie, and her male counterpart is known as Papa or Uncle.

Before explaining who and what these aakhu are and why they are so unique. I must first state that there is a lot of misunderstanding about these two spirits particularly La Madama because of cultural appropriation. The other part is due to lack of understanding, so I decided to put my two-cents in about this spirit.

Before I begin, I must remind you that most African Americans never had a name for our spiritual tradition. That's right! Most Black people never said they practice hoodoo or rootwork because they were Protestants and hoodoo and rootwork was looked upon as being witchcraft. Now, that does not mean they didn't use herbs, roots, sticks, oils, etc. They just never had a name for it. The naming of our tradition most likely was some crap that white people started and unfortunately (like so many things), it stuck out of continual use. I am telling you this to give you a little background on how cultural appropriation has been historically used and why such ambiguity exists today.

So, who is La Madama?

Well with respect to those in the various Caribbean Spiritist traditions, La Madama generally speaking is the spirit of a black Cuban or black Puerto Rican woman who was most likely a Palera, a female practitioner of Palo Mayombe a.k.a Regla de Kongo (Kongo Rule) or Santera (a female practitioner of Lucumi a.k.a. Santeria). La Madamas are therefore, the spirits of the dead who were enslaved women, who typically were depicted as house servants wearing a gingham skirt or apron and head scarf.

Now. That being said, it must be remembered that when the Africans were taken to the Caribbean, many of them were able to keep their religious beliefs relatively intact. However, the Africans taken to North America were not able to accomplish this feat. This means that many of the same Africans who were taken to North America, who had similar beliefs and practices as those taken to the Caribbean but no religious structure, performed similar task in North America.

In other words, there were many enslaved African women who performed similar tasked in North America as the enslaved

African women in the Caribbean. In fact, archeological and historical research has found that "at least one-third" of the enslaved African American population were of Kongo-Angolan descent. Remember, according to historical records, the first enslaved Africans brought to North America were from the Kongo-Angolan region, which means most of the enslaved Africans practiced a similar faith as their enslaved Caribbean kin prior to the Second Great Awakening, when enslaved African Americans converted to Christianity – particularly Baptist and Methodist denominations – in droves around the 1820s. To put it bluntly, think of Palo Mayombe with no rules being practiced for at least two hundred years (1619 is the first time the English documented African slaves arriving on a Portuguese ship).

Now, unlike in some parts of the Caribbean (and Brazil) where the African culture was partially "adored", colorism was tolerated to some degree (until it was able to be squashed appropriately) and African heritage celebrated. In North America, the African was not adored and everything considered African in nature was ridiculed. In an effort to justify slavery and the continual subjugation of African people and their descendants. Racist whites took every aspect of African American culture and created stereotypical images of it. Let me make it plain. For example, in Puerto Rico where bomba is celebrated and in Cuba where children are taught rhumba. In the United States to justify slavery similar dances such as the ring shout were ridiculed and called shuffling and jiving (a term still used today). In Puerto Rico and Cuba were Chango Macho is celebrated and honored with his rich dark skin and proud smile to symbolize victory, domination and triumph. In the United States similar images would be ridiculed and called sambos, golliwops, etc. Chango's rich smile would be used to sell toothpaste! Our strong, wise and powerful African fathers who abhorred slavery and given the opportunity would revolt (see the list of Slave Revolts) were used as a propaganda tool to illustrate how happy black folks were to be slaves, and the healing memories of African mothers were reduced to selling damn pancakes!

In other words, every positive image African Americans had was perverted and used as a psychological weapon to ridicule every aspect of our culture. And finally, broadcasted and publicized all over the world to convince others that people of African descent were inferior to Westerners. As a result, this same disrespect continues to exist and is commercialized to this day. Every time you see an elderly black woman usually wearing a headscarf who is robust, it is a reminder of this painful period. This has resulted in many of our spirit guides existing in a type of limbo. True spiritists would understand this!

All of that changed when Cubans and Puerto Ricans began coming to the United States and sharing their spiritual experience. For instance, I will never forget the time I saw my padrino's La Madama standing next to his Ellegua. When I asked him who was she? He told me that she La Madama and that she was his Ellegua's wife. I wished I had asked him for more details, such as was she a spirit of a former Santera or Palera but I didn't. The fact that he said that his Madama was Ellegua's wife was interesting in itself. In fact, the only time I even heard of an Ellegua having a wife was in the Brazilian Macumba tradition where Exu's (the Ellegua equivalent) wife was named Pomba Gira. Whatever the case, seeing my padrino's La Madama was the first time I saw Aunt Jemima in a positive and powerful light.

So, African Americans who honored La Madama were actually honoring the spirits of African women, many of whom were Kongo-Angolan descendants. They chose to call these spirits La Madama because it is more honorable and respectful than the name racist whites gave them which was "Mammy."

Now, with respect to those from the Caribbean Spiritists, maybe they should not be called Las Madamas, but technically speaking they are Madamas. For this reason, I refer to them as Mommas and Aunties and the elderly men as Papa or Uncles. They represent the wisdom, knowledge and faith of the Fathers and Mothers, Uncles and Aunties, Grandfathers and Grandmothers.

To me they also represent the spirits of the Africans who resisted slavery by creating new and ingenious ways to survive using holistic models. From this perspective they are symbols of the first Africans who were brought to the Americas. As a result, their energy continues to exist in the African American community, which is the reason we call elderly men and women out of respect Papa (Big Dad) or Uncle and Big Momma or Auntie.

These aakhu are seen as the spirit guides who belong to one of the various African tribes that were brought to North America and forced into slavery. Since everything has to be balanced, I believe that we each have a Papa and Momma cultural aakhu that will dominate and orchestrate the efforts of the other cultural aakhu. The Papa and Momma cultural aakhu may be from the same tribal nation or different. For instance, both of my Papa and Momma aakhu are of Kongo-Angolan descent, which is heavily reflected in this work. However, it is possible to have a Papa and Momma from two different tribal nations. Like your Papa could be Wolof and your Big Ma Kongo, and so on.

In Kongo thinking most of the images of these spirits are always depicted in white because it corresponds to the Ra Atum-Luvemba moment or setting sun, the symbol of elders and those nearing death. The color white is also a reflection of Osar's glorious Underworld or KAMTA, which is imagined being all-white.

To honor these aakhu, any image of elderly African Americans can be used to honor these aakhu.

They are fond of strong black coffee, cornbread, calas (rice fritter), strong teas, porridges, pound cake, cigars (or pipe tobacco) and other simple items that elderly people enjoy.

How Do We Connect with Spirits?

Some aakhu stay with us for a short period of time, while others stay with us for all of our life because of a soul connection. Some aakhu help you to overcome certain issues that are going on in your life and when you understand the lesson they will leave. Some of these spirits, if you do not have a strong head, will lead you into their world and rescue you just in the nick of time. For instance, a lot of young people are still influenced by the deceased rapper 2 Pac because he helped them to rise above certain obstacles, they faced in their life in regard to police brutality and other social ills. Some of them followed in 2Pac's footsteps with similar consequences but they all consider him a guide who helps those in the underworld.

It was the deceased rapper Ole' Dirty Bastard (ODB) of Wu-Tang who helped me to rise above a certain grimy situation, at one point of my life. But anyone who knows about ODB knows that he was really into some strong drugs. Listening to his music would catapult me into that world. Thankfully, I learned the lesson I needed from him, so` I have no need to venture down that path. Every-now and then, he will pop up and I will hear one of his songs in my ears and ODB would come to town, signifying me to watch out, be on my toes and *"Protect Ya Neck!"* This aakhu was associated with my historical aakhu.

Now all aakhu are not the same. I have two examples to illustrate this point. First, since I was raised in the church and my father at the time was an assistant pastor when I was younger. I felt a special connection with Malcolm X (El Hajj Malik Shabazz) whose father was also a preacher. Like Malcolm, after seeing the hypocrisy of Christians, I turned my back on God because I believed that God did not care. Although I did not delve as deep as Malcolm had into the criminal world, I was at its' doorsteps. My confusion about God led me to consider converting to Islam but I stopped short because dancing was considered a sin. Malcolm had helped me to see that if I had joined Islam, I was basically converting from one dogmatic religion to another that demonized African cultural expressions.

Malcolm had also helped me to see that the Supreme Being does not give a damn what religion we are in, or if we believe in God or not. Only egotistical people care about what religion you are or are not in. The Supreme Being is not going to cease filling your lungs with air because you are Baptist, Buddhist, a Muslim, etc. It was these two points that led me from calling him Malcolm X to just Malcolm, as a sincere friend. Please note that everyone may not have had this same type of experience but these are a couple of things that Malcolm told me. There were a few more lessons that Malcolm taught me but these were the most important that I needed. After I learned them, he backed away like a parent allowing their child to walk for the first time alone. Now, he is still in my life but not as much as he had used to be.

My second story is that I remembered I had a couple of my uncles who were taking martial arts from a man from Japan. I remembered every time we went to this dojo (training place for martial arts), we had to bow several times to honor the sensei's teachers before actually entering the area where they actually trained. It dawned on me that even though the sensei's teachers were not related to my uncles. His deceased teachers were imagined as helping new students learn their martial arts tradition. In other words, they were spirit guides for new and old students, which means spirit guides are the spirits of the dead that exist outside of our biological circle.

That being said, you are responsible for the spirits who you attract. No one (alive or dead) has the right to tell you who will attract and honor. The only way you are going to attract negative and evil spirits to you is by regularly focusing on negative and evil thoughts. If you do not want to attract these negative energies, then you have to stop engaging in low energy activities and behaviors.

I remember, I used to love watching ghost and haunted house movies but the more I worked with honoring my ancestors. The less I enjoyed this genre of films because I realized ghost movies were highly sensational. Most of these movies are not focused on trying to help people to understand the nature of the spiritual realm. They are solely focused on frightening people based upon the ignorance. It also seemed like many of these horror movies were created to deter people from honoring their ancestors or at least understanding the nature of the spirit world. So, I stopped watching them and since them, my experience with my ancestors has grown.

How Do Helping Spirits (Aakhu) Assist Us?

There are many ways that the aakhu can help us because unlike other spiritual traditions and religions that usually requires that one adopts and change their beliefs, in order to succeed in the hierarchy of the tradition. Our aakhu accept us for who we are. They love us regardless. They do not care what we believe or do, so long as they like elder family members are cared for. Care for them, and they will care for you.

However, they can be a bit demanding. If they had certain ethics and principles that they lived by. They expect you to live by those same ethics and principles as well because it was their ethics and principles that made it possible for you to be here today. It is true that some traditions become outdated and useless due to changing times, and therefore obsolete. However, this does not mean that ancestral traditions are obsolete. Many people believe that they can live any kind of way, and it is true. You have the right to live your life as you want to, but if you want blessings from your aakhu. You have to live a righteous life.

I remember once I was having the hardest time trying to implement a practice in my life. I mean it did not matter what I did, I kept running into roadblocks until one evening something said, "Explain why you want to do this." So, I went to my het aakhu (ancestor altar) and explained why and how I thought a certain practice could benefit the family. After doing so, I felt a burden lifted and things worked themselves out with ease. I learned a very valuable lesson that evening about my biological aakhu, which is that they will only give a 100 percent if it benefits the entire family.

The other aakhu that assist us who may not be related to us biologically are connected to us on a soul level. When the Africans were enslaved and their families were dismantled and sold like property all over the United States. A lot of adopted families were created. As a result, many people were cared for people by loved ones who were not biologically related. For instance, my father had a pretty rough childhood. At age 14, he was kicked out of the house by his father and forced to live on the streets. His Aunt Liz and Uncle James were the ones who took him in, which later I learned were not biologically related to him. They were the ones who provided him with the best instruction during his teenage years because they connected with him on a soul level. Today, they continue to frequent the het aakhu because of this soul connection.

How Do You Talk to Your Spirits?

Many of us from a religious background had been taught to pray every time we need a spiritual blessing, but what I have found is that this is not necessary. Our spirits are our spirits. They know us. They know what we do and who we are, so I personally do not see a need to be formal. Out of respect and to set the mood I may say the *Lord's Prayer* or *Psalms 23rd* but, other than. I do not really believe in praying to my ancestors. Praying always reminds me of when I was a teenager at church, begging and tarrying for the Holy Ghost to descend upon me.

I do not believe that my I am worthy and that my spirits think I am worthy, so I do not need to beg for anything. I respectfully talk to my spirits just like I would talk to my friends. Spirits are at a vantage point because they do not have a physical body and are therefore, are not bound by time and space. However, we (the living) have a vantage over them because we have a physical body, which gives us the ability to experience life. In other words, spirits are not superior to you but at the same time, we are not superior over them. We both have something to gain from each other, which is why the relationship with spirits is more like a partnership. If you keep this in mind, instead of thinking of them as being your superiors. You will have a very powerful experience.

To talk to your spirits follow these basic rules:

1. Remember that most spirit guides were one upon a time people, so they had likes and dislikes. When you call upon a spirit you may not establish a rapport immediately because you may be doing something that they find offensive. This is what has led people to believe that the spirit guide chooses whom they want to work with.
2. Second, for this reason if you choose to work with a spirit you need to read that spirit's story. Understand their history. This will help you avoid trickster spirits of Set who will gas you up, play on your fears and inflate your ego. Your aakhu will not lead you astray. Review how helping spirits communicate to us.
3. Last but not least, always be skeptical about what spirits tell you. Benevolent spirits understand that just like you would not trust a stranger off the street with your life, you are not expected to trust spirits the same way without building a rapport. Hence, the saying "try the spirit" and see if what they are telling you is true. Benevolent spirits will never encourage you to do something that is out of your comfort zone. They are not going to tell you to perform surgery if you have no idea how the human body works and never went to medical school. However, malevolent spirits would because they do not care how they get energy, so long as they get it. Always be skeptical about what spirits tell you until it has been proven to be an observable truth. You will know when you are receiving sound advice because it will resonate with you and make sense like a Eureka moment. As always, test it.

Ancestral Curses & Generational Problems

If you were not raised in a culture that venerates ancestors, it is usually difficult for you to comprehend how and why your ancestors would trouble you. You will spend a lot of time trying to intellectually comprehend this entire concept and the whole concept regarding the spiritual realm. We have to remember that we are not just thinking beings but feeling beings:

1. Several members within the family have the exact same or similar problems. For instance, a mother was a teen mom and she have several daughters who also are teen mothers. A grandfather suffers from alcoholism, his son suffers from alcoholism, and his grandson suffers from alcoholism or some other form of substance abuse.
2. You cannot find a rational explanation for the phenomenon and/or modern science cannot explain an easily treatable condition such as unexplainable and sudden illnesses like chest pains, skin rashes, etc.

One of the added benefits of venerating your ancestors is that they will assist you in healing ancestral curses. An ancestral curse is a negative pattern that affects succeeding generations and sometimes called generational curses. For instance, if a grandmother had a teen pregnancy, her daughter had a teen pregnancy, and then her granddaughters had a teen pregnancy. This is probably due to an ancestral curse. This is not the only way ancestral curses can affect us. It is possible for an aakhu suffering from guilt and shame can carry transfer that energy to us. Other times, an aakhu can be cursed from someone and it affects us. Through venerating one's ancestors, it is possible to uncover cyclic patterns and cleanse ourselves of them.

There are a number of reasons ancestral problems or curses can occur. The two most common reasons are simply because when the ancestor passed away, they had unfulfilled desires. For instance, the aakhu is upset because they living descendant is not using their inheritance according to their aakhu's wishes. Another unfulfilled desire is that the aakhu wants things to be done in a particular manner than the way the living relative is choosing.

Also, aapepu who have unfulfilled desires may take an opportunity to fulfill their addiction through their living descendant. The second reason is because the aapepu is trying to draw attention to them because they are unable to ascend to a higher level. Therefore, to remedy this problem we venerate the ancestors.

Lesson Three: Working with the Honorable Dead

Building a Het Aakhu (Ancestor and Spirit Guide Altar)

What needs to be understood about ancestor veneration is that we do not worship the dead. We honor, respect and ask them for guidance. Presently, I have been honoring and working with my ancestors and spirit guides off and on for approximately 20 years, but I still would not claim that I am an authority on the subject. Lately ancestor veneration has become a popular subject. It is presently one of the hottest spiritual fads. What people needs to understand is that ancestor veneration for people of color is not a fad, a magickal practice, a ceremonial rite to prepare you to work with the spirits of the dead, etc. No. For people of color – particularly African Americans - ancestral veneration is a spiritual practice that was adopted because our cultural ancestral practice was suppressed. The purpose of honoring our ancestors was to get insight from them in order to improve the quality of our life. They helped us to better understand how to use the powers of the Creator.

Ancestor veneration is a personal spiritual practice, which means that it differs from person to person. I have heard people say that you should not get angry with your ancestors because this is a sign of disrespect, but I have never experienced this. If your ancestors are supposed to be family, then just because they have no physical body does not mean you cannot fuss at them. Sometimes you want to stop talking to them all together because things get frustrating. Why? Because it is like having a real relationship with a living person. This action is sometimes required to weed your sacred space of negative ancestral spirits who might have cropped up around you.

Understand that your true ancestors will not abandon you. They will always be around even if you do not physically honor them because they are within you.

The format I found that best suits my needs was Espiritismo Cruzado (Crossed Spiritism), which was taught to me by Papa. According to Papa Espiristimo Cruzado was a good and healthy tradition because:

1) It could be used by anyone because it was a flexible and did not have a dogma.
2) It could easily be used by both solitary and group practitioners, and.
3) It is adaptable to anyone's beliefs, so as one's understanding grows, the boveda grows as well, and last but not least.

When I was recovering from my illness, I experimented with several ways of honoring my ancestors. During that time, I still kept my ancestors in my mind even though I did not physically honor them by giving them light, water and other offerings. In other words, I still respected them. I still missed them and I still loved them, so I know that they understood everything that I was experiencing.

It was during my recovery that I decided to fully adopt the Espiritismo Cruzado format because it was the only format that helped me to remember that our Osar rests on our right shoulder and Set on our left shoulder. In other words, it was the only format that would ensure that we fulfill our purpose.

We as human beings need to constantly be reminded that our Osar and Set are battling within and the one who wins is the one we choose to follow. In other words, we need to constantly be reminded that we are responsible for our own salvation, which means what we do with our life is solely in our hands. It is very easy for us to forget this and really simple for us to fall into the trap of blaming others for our shortcomings. Our ancestors and spirit guides, like loving parents want us to grow. In fact, the more we learn and evolve, the more they learn and evolve, but not all of our ancestors are in a position to help us. So, I wanted to know what ancestors are and what actually are ancestors, spirit guides and negative spirits, and what the difference is.

For this reason, everything within our sacred space should be at eye-level (or below) to remind us and our spirits, that like Hru working with his father Osar, we are communicating for a common cause. In this relationship, the spirits are not superior over the living nor are the living more superior to the spirit, which is a Western-thinking mindset. In our sacred space, the spirits are in the trenches because the living are in the trenches. We (the living and the spirits) are therefore on the same level working to accomplish a similar goal like Hru and Osar.

When we create sacred space, we like Oset and Nebhet who after finding a "member" of Osar's body erected a shrine in his honor, also become a "member" dedicated to Osar's return[2]. This sacred space is a visual indicator to you and the spirits that you are willing to enter into agreement with benevolent spirits in order to improve each other's' fate. In other words, it is built to thank them for their assistance and illustrate that you are willing to enter into an agreement with them, so that you can assist each other in your spiritual growth.

Sacred space or an altar makes the aakhu feel welcomed and illustrates to them that they have not been forgotten. In this

---

[2] Please note that I am speaking of the Spirit of Osar's metaphysical and metaphorical return, not his or some other mystical savior's literal return or rapture.

tradition is called a het aakhu, which is Kemetic for "house of or for (ancestral) spirits." The het aakhu or het (for short) serves numerous purposes for the spiritually minded. Keeping in mind that our universe is mental, the acts as a meeting place between you and your spirits. However, from a psychological perspective the het is one of the most powerful tools for spiritual development because since our sahu (subconscious) does not distinguish between time and space. Any idea that is impressed upon it for a long period of time is interpreted as being real and in the present. The het therefore symbolizes the various compartments within our mind, which makes it easier to manifest whatever changes we desire.

Finally, the het also is a sacrificial table where offerings are made. As we read in Part II of this book, our universe is composed of two realities, which consists of ten dimensions. The tenth dimension or lowest dimension is the physical reality and it has a strong gravitational pull. Whenever we need assistance from our aakhu (ancestors and spirit guides) and netcharu (guardian spirits) to reach another level. It is like shooting a rocket out in space, it requires a lot of energy or a lot of force to accomplish that goal. Therefore, offerings are placed on the het in order for it to be transformed into energy used for a higher purpose.

The het used in Kamta are two tiered (or leveled) either in a bookshelf form or step form to provide a surface for the aakhu below and a place for the netcharu. To build the first level or step of the het:

Step 1: Choose a location: Find a location in your home where you can meditate and/or pray. It is best to place your het (altar) in a quiet location out of the view of passerby's and set it against one wall. If space is limited, you can choose to place your het in the closet or some other secluded area within your home. Although, it is ideal that your het face either the south or southeast direction, it is not necessary since the real het occurs within your mind. Whichever space you choose hang either an ankh, bare crucifix, a star or a symbol of the aabit (lunar Eye of Ra), etc. to represent the midnight moment of the sun, Amun Ra.

Step 2: Choose an altar surface: Since the spiritual realm is imagined as being similar to the physical realm in the sense that the living has a home and places to work. Ideally the het should have two tiers or two levels with the first (or lower) level providing a home for your aakhu (ancestral spirits and spirit guides), and the second (or higher) level is for your netcharu (guardian spirits), which provides a sense of employment. Therefore, it is best to build your het on a low bookshelf or stacks of boxes. If this is not possible, a desk or table can be used to represent the second tier and a thin plank of wood can be used for the first level. Whichever surface you choose, the second tier should not be higher than eye level (and within reach) to indicate that the netcharu are within reach and a reminder that Set created this obstacle. But high enough to allow candles to burn freely on the lower tier.

In addition, you may also want to place a chair and/or cushion in front of your het.

Step 3: Preparing the surface: With a mild soap detergent, clean the surface (if using a table the legs also) of physical debris. Allow it to air-dry. Then, place decorative white cloths on the bottom and top tiers to symbolize Osar's purity and the bone memory of all who came before us, since Osar is the ruler of this realm. White is also a nice neutral color that can be used for building altars.

Step 4: Creating a Spiritual Border: On the bottom tier place, white seashells, white rocks, etc. around the edge to mark where the spiritual and physical realm meet. If using a step form het, place the seashells or rocks around the entire edge of the het. Seashells are preferred because the analogy is that they naturally protect what is precious within. Also, the outside of the seashell creates a border indicating that what is within is hidden.

Step 5: Honoring Maa, Shu & Tefnut forces: Shu is the Kemetic Yang principle and Tefnut is the Kemetic Yin principle, together these two primordial forces ensure that Maa always exist. Shu, the hot, fiery, masculine principles always marches in first and is followed by his twin sister Tefnut, the cool, watery feminine principle. Shu must come in first to clear or burn the way of debris, weeds, etc. so that Tefnut can provide the nurturance to sustain growth and sustenance. Both Shu and Tefnut are inseparable, so to represent Maa, Shu and Tefnut.

Place a crucifix or ankh in the center of the het to symbolize Maa. On the left-hand side of the symbol of Maa place an icon (figurine, picture, statue, etc.) to represent the Papa or Uncle Aakhu (symbolizing the masculine energy). On the right of the Maa place an icon to represent the Momma or Auntie Aakhu (symbolizing the feminine energy). In addition, you can also place an image of Osar overlooking your aakhu since this Osar's realm in the first place. However, this is not necessary.

Step 6: Symbolizing the Nine Guardians of Kemet: Assemble one large goblet of water in the center of the het. Next place four glasses of cool water on the left and four glasses of cool water on the right. This should give you a total of nine receptacles of cool clear water. These nine receptacles symbolize the nine major spiritual forces, the nine spiritual clans, the nine cycles, the gestation period and the nine divisions. The nine glasses can be setup as follows per your inspiration. The following setups are formats I have learned from experimenting.

Basic Glass Set-up

Glass Set-up for Attack

Glass Set-up for Defense

Now that you have a general understanding how our universe operates; it should be noted that different spirits will come and go in and out of our homes every day. Many of these aakhu will have no relation to us but can still offer assistance. The goblet and glasses of water are placed on the het to inform these passing spirits of the netcharu who fought to unify Kemet.

The arrangement can be seen as like providing directions to spiritual pilgrim. When these aakhu see the altar, they will immediately understand that the het is for spiritual elevation. At that time, they can either decide to work or move on.

Step 7: Remembering Your Aakhu: Think about your aakhu and how they lived when they were physically alive. Think about the things that they like and how they were an inspiration to you. With fond memories of your aakhu in mind, place photos of your male ancestors you wish to honor on the left side, and photos of your female ancestors on the right side of the het. Caution: Do not place photos of living individuals on the het because it would indicate that they

Place items that your aakhu would enjoy next to their images like a strong coffee or strong teas (no sugar) in a white coffee cup. For instance, my grandmother liked spearmint flavor chewing gum so a pack of chewing gum is on the het next to her image. One of my aakhu enjoyed loose leaf chewing tobacco. Basically, you want to create a familiar setting for the aakhu by placing their favorite knickknacks on the het such as foods and tools.

Perfumes, colognes and other fragrances can be poured in a small glass jar and left near their images. Also, things that they used can also be placed on the het near their image. If they smoke a pack of cigarettes is left so that they can enjoy. If they enjoyed reading the bible, then place a bible for them. It is important to remember that the items placed on the het are for their benefit.

These are the things that helped them in life to help you. Many of our recent aakhu were Christians and there was something in it that helped them to become who they are remembered for. So, it is disrespectful to not honor their memory because you disagree with their choice of religion. Provide for them the things they need to progress, so that they can assist you as well.

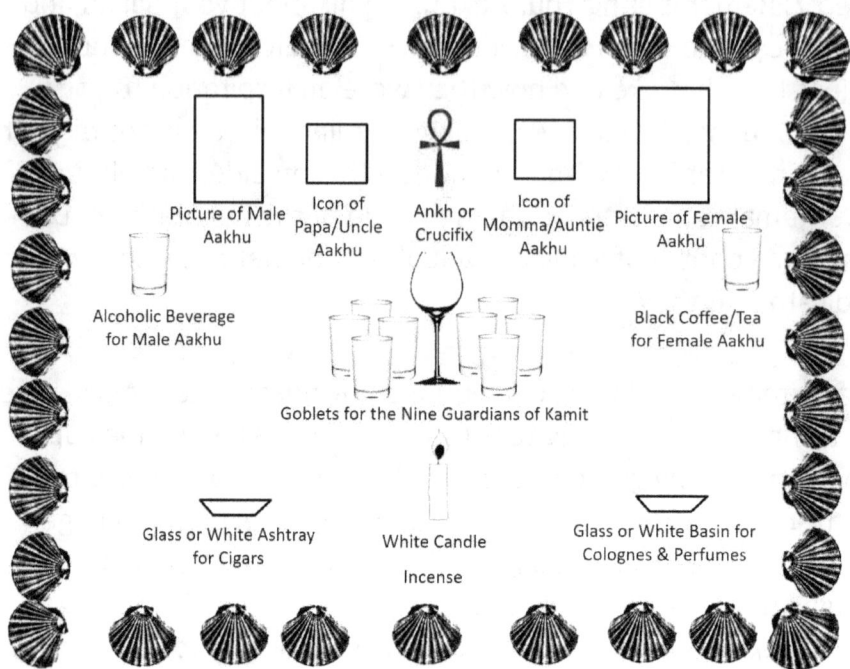

Incense Burner

In addition, you can also add glass ashtrays and/or white painted clay bowls to keep hot ashes and hot wax spills from causing fires. These containers can also be filled with sand to prevent them from becoming too hot and scorching the surface. **Remember to never leave candles and incense unattended or near flammable objects.**

I choose to burn incense on the outside of the het so that anything placed on the het can be smoked and purified.

Some important things to consider:
- Always refresh your glasses on a weekly basis. Also, try to keep your glasses on your het full of fresh cool water. This will prevent the glasses from getting hard water stains. If your glasses do get hard water stains, simply fill them with

white vinegar and let them sit for 20 minutes. Once the stains have been removed, wash the glasses with a mild dish water detergent, rinse and allow them to air dry before placing them back on the het.
- In some cultures, only the male ancestors are honored because it is believed they are responsible for furthering the family lineage. An extension of this belief is that ancestor veneration is performed by the men or the head male of the household. If there is no father, then the eldest male. This was to ensure that the ancestors were always taken care of. Due to Western influence these traditional rules have been skewed. The aakhu will be pleased to receive any type of assistance. However, married couples should observe how they want to proceed in regard to honoring their aakhu. It may be required that the husband and wife share an ancestral het or maintain separate hets. Follow your intuition and use divination to verify messages.
- Remember that the het is yours to do whatsoever you will. You are in complete control of it. No one has the right to tell you what to or not to place on your het. You have the right to add or subtract from you het as you feel. If something does not feel right move it. If you like something, then add it to your het. Allow your intuition to be your guide but always be aware of the purpose. For instance, do not just put an item on your het because someone has done it. Research it and experiment with it first before adopting it, to see how it will benefit you.
- Play drumming and chanting music to honor the various African ethnicities and let them know that you remember them.

Remember, there is no right or wrong way to honor your aakhu. The wrong way is the way that does not feel right to you. That being said, there are only two rules you must follow when working with the aakhu:

1. First, never let your het become dilapidated. Meaning do not let it get run down. As soon as there is a sign of decay, immediately clean the het and refresh it. If need be, avoid placing objects on the het that will cause the het to quickly decay. For instance, I only place flowers on my het when I really need to because as soon as the petals begin to fall it is hard to clean up sometimes. So I avoid placing flowers on the het. This also means do not let your het become a resting place for ordinary things like your car keys, bills, etc. On place objects on the het that you want imbued with spiritual power.
2. Do not place photos of the living on the het or lay items like keys, papers, etc. Remember, this is your aakhus' home, which means whatever you place on it, belongs to them.

Weekly Ritual to Honor the Aakhu

As I have mentioned previously, ancestor veneration from a shamanic perspective is practiced different from other traditions. This is because we view our ancestors and spirit guides as existing within and outside of us. In other words, the memories of our aakhu can also be found in nature. So to work with your aakhu, you must understand that their sphere of awareness is anything regarding the family. The following ritual is how I venerate my aakhu:

- Step 1: Light incense (frankincense, frankincense & myrrh, sandalwood, etc.), place on the outside of the het aakhu (ancestral altar) and pass all of the items offered to the aakhu through the smoke. The idea is that each time you

offer something to the aakhu it is purified as it passes through the curtain of incense smoke.
- Step 2: Assemble the nine glasses on the het aakhu to resemble a tribunal and pour cool water into each glass begin with the largest goblet. (See glasses setup above).
- Step 3: Recite a prayer. Since I recognize Osar as the Lord within me, I recite the *Lord's Prayer* and/or *Psalms 23rd*, which are very both good general prayers used for invocation. It will remind you that you are Hru (regardless of your gender) and that you are at war with Set. Remember Osar is the personification of our BA (Superconscious), which is the divine patriarch similar to Abraham, Moses, Jesus, etc. Also, give thanks for all of the blessings that you acquired. This is a perfect time to express your gratitude.
- Step 4: Ask the Lord to bless and strengthen them, then offer a white candle to your aakhu.
- Step 5: Offer your aakhu favorites items to strengthen their soul such as strong black coffee (no sugar), tea (no sugar), a shot of liquor (rum, vodka, whiskey, etc.), food (with no salt), fresh flowers, etc. Say, "I honor (your ancestor's names who you remember). I honor all those remembered and forgotten. I honor all those who were companions and friends associated with my aakhu."
- Step 6: Say, "Thank your aakhu for their assistance and sharing their wisdom." Note that if you have any cultural aakhu (Big Dad spirit, Uncle Spirit, Big Momma Spirit, Auntie Spirit, Black Hawk Spirit, etc.) whom you are inspired to honor. If you have their icon (figurine, statue, doll, etc.), light a candle and pay homage to them for helping you to spiritually grow. For instance, "Thank you Black Hawk for watching and preventing intrusions," and so on.

- Step 7: Allow the candle to burn out completely. Repeat steps 3 – 6 on a day that is most convenient for you.

It is important to understand that you can at any time focus on the positive aspects of your aakhu and either give them libations by pouring water or liquor to them, which saying their names. This can be performed daily or weekly. In addition, you can also remember your aakhu by offering them a portion of your meal.

Now, culturally and historically most African Americans do not categorize family members into classes such as nuclear family, immediate family, extended family, etc. Grandma and grandad are not considered separate family unit because they live in another house in another part of the community, state or country. Family is considered family. Period.

For example, in my family, the rule was if you lived under the same cultural roof, you followed the same cultural rules because you were family. There was no such thing as step brothers and step-sisters in my family. No one even used the term. Everyone was considered family and was treated as such.

When a family member stepped outside the cultural and historical guidelines and engage in activities or behaviors that may cause harm to the family collective. Someone within the family would either pull you to the side or put you in check, or several other members put you in check. If the offense was really bad, you were ousted because of your self-destructive and offensive behavior. This did not mean that you were kicked out of the family. Family members simply limited their interaction with you until you changed and ceased put your own interest above the family.

This is important to understand because a lot of people think that in these contemporary times that they can do whatsoever they please. They see people on these reality shows doing whatever and think they can live the same way. It is just not true. What these people do not understand is that what you see on television and the movies is entertainment.

Now, when I say people think that they can do whatsoever they please. I mean marry whomever they want and live their life any kind of way. Sure, you have the right to do whatever you want but if you want the protection and assistance of your ancestors you cannot.

Remember, our ancestors continued to practice their indigenous beliefs for at least two hundred years while they were captives in this country. Then, for the next two hundred or so years, they practiced a 'syncretization' or Creole version of Christianity, which was infused with their indigenous beliefs. This means that our family structure was most likely established by a second generation African American, who was somewhat familiar with African customs and beliefs, and the hypocrisy of the "New World." These are spirits that overlook our family. These are the ancestral spirits who set the cultural norm that your family follows, which means if you are having family issues. It is most likely because you have offended these ancestral spirits and they have withdrawn their support.

Please understand that I am not trying to incite fear in you about your ancestors, but you must remember. That spirits were once upon a time living and breathing people who had likes and dislikes. Unlike the Supreme Being, they can turn their back on you if they do not approve of what you are doing because they have that right.

Let me give you an example.

There was a family member of mine whose wife was not familiar with our family customs. She came from a family where children can call their parents by their first name. Essentially this means that the children are on the same level as the parent. Anyway, one day she got upset and raised her voice at my father because of something she disagrees with that he said. It was very disrespectful and several family members had commented that she needed to apologize, which she refused. Some family members had even reached out and talked to her side of the family to get her to right her wrong. Again, she refused. Finally, I took the issue to my aakhu and let them deal with it.

Several months had passed and all of a sudden, this family member began having family problems in his home. There were small little accidents that occurred and other little mishaps. Then, that is when this family member told his wife that she needed to apologize to my father. Eventually, she finally humbled herself and apologized.

The lesson to be learned by this is that Maa is not about right and wrong as so many people think. Maa is about equality and equity. My family member's wife had the right to disagree with my father and be upset for the remark he made. She did not have the right to disrespect him especially when she was not being disrespected. Her actions created an imbalance result in their family not receiving protection from the aakhu. The imbalance was created because if someone had treated her parents as such, she would not have appreciated either. Her disrespect and refusal to apologize was driven by her ego (Set), thus justifying the aakhu's reaction.

One of the ways to work with your aakhu is by telling them whatever is troubling you. If you want, you can write it out on a sheet of paper. Then leave the matter in their hands. When the aakhu fulfill your request, it is important that you express your gratitude by giving them an offering.

For instance, say you want to ask your Papa to give you insight on how to improve the rapport of the men in your family. You would petition him and tell him what the problem is. Then, ask him to provide you with a solution. When your petition has been met, offer him a lit white candle, a shot of rum or a cigar, or something that you think he may favor.

Final Note on Making Offerings to Spirits

The whole purpose of giving spirits offerings is because the currency in the spiritual realm is energy. Spirits are given offerings because offering give them energy on the other side. When people keep a spirits' memory alive, it gives them spiritual currency or energy in the spiritual realm. When a memorial is built, where they are given flowers, toys, candies, vigils, etc. This gives the spirit energy. Also, items that spirits enjoyed while alive such as perfume, books they liked to read like the bible, etc. also gives them energy. Remember, you are placing items that they liked, not what you liked. This is the reason why if they were a Christian you put the bible on the het.

Now, the spirits are not able to use any of these physical things but it is the gesture and the energy behind it that empowers them.

In recent years, there has been a lot of talk about ancestor money called Chinese hell money or heaven notes. Story goes that when Westerners encountered the Chinese folk practice of burning money, the Westerners in an attempt to discourage the Chinese from honoring their ancestors, tried to demonize it by claiming their ancestors were in hell. The Chinese unmoved by the Western mockery, adopted the term hell and used it to empower the practice, so the idea was adopted that they were paying for their ancestors to get out of hell. Said another way, they were paying for their ancestors to advance out of hell.

It is an interesting concept and take on ancestor veneration, however when I first learned of this practice ten years ago. It did not work for me because I never believed that my ancestors were in hell in the first place. Many of us believed that our ancestors had gone to heaven even if we did not know how they got there because Christianity failed to explain this. These were beliefs that were brought from Africa, so our ancestors were always believed to be taken care of. Most people never believed that they needed our help but that we needed their help since they were closer to God.

In lieu of our beliefs, giving spirits who are closer to God money or any offering never made a lot of sense to me. However, giving them offerings in exchange for their assistance does because most spirits are familiar with *quid pro quo*, which is doing something for something. In other words, most spirits would prefer to work for their offerings then receive charity. That being said, offering spirits fake money in exchange for a service rendered does not have the same effect as giving them real money. Spirits want the same things that they used in life in death. Another way to think of it is that if you can use it, they cannot use it.

A lot of Yoruba spirits are familiar with using cowrie shells for money, so this becomes an offering that they are familiar with. This symbolism is not applicable for many of us in the US because we never used cowrie shells in this fashion. So, if I give my aakhu a handful of cowrie shells, I imagine they would be like "What the hell is this?" However, I give them something they loved or could use, I will get a better response. For instance, I have had better results giving my aakhu actual real money because it is something, they are familiar with and they can use. How do they use it? I have no idea but they do. In fact, I remember I learned about this practice by observing several people offer wads of cash to their ancestors in order to keep them from making mistakes.

Again, why does it work? Because it is like making a sacrifice where you release the energy from this world and put it in their world or the spirit world. Once you take anything (food, drink, money, etc.) out of this world and refuse to consume it or spend it for a physical purpose. You have transformed a physical thing and made it sacred by making it spiritual. For instance, when you cease to consume food or drink, hence fasting. You have just offered the food and drink to the spiritual realm, which pays you back with spiritual knowledge and power.

Anything can be made sacred by giving it to your spirits in exchange for a petition answered, but the real offering consists of you giving something that you use. Rest assure, you do not have to give up your first born or your soul. Your spirits don't want that because they can't use it. What spirits want the most is time and energy, which is the reason the things that they favor the most are food, drink and money because it is all about faith.

Please note, that it is not necessary that you put yourself in the poor house trying to make an offering. If you cannot afford to give something. Give what you can instead. Again, your spirits need you, just as much as you need them.

FOUR:
The Guardian Spirits

If you say the term Kemet to most people. They will tell you about the pyramids, the Great Sphinx of Giza and their so-called esoteric philosophy, but what most people refuse to talk about out of fear; is the Kemetic peoples' philosophy regarding the spirits of the dead.

The Kemetic people believed that when we physically die, the Ab soul survives the death experience but loses its' physical body (its vessel to move around and experience life on earth). In other words, when a person dies and loses their physical body, they can no longer experience what we call life. For instance, with no ears they cannot hear and enjoy music; with no body, they cannot feel pleasure or pain; without a mouth, they cannot taste food or drinks; with no nose, they cannot smell; with no eyes they cannot even see. They simply just exist in a boring realm, so two extraordinary things occurred:

1) The newly deceased goes to the underworld, which is a place of heavenly reward (that was initially for the royalty and later for all after the Middle Ages). But since the underworld was like a lifeless retirement home, in the sense that you could not experience anything because you did not have a physical body. The newly deceased was forced to roam the earth without a body hungry and thirsty.

2) This meant that the love ones of the newly deceased needed to capture their soul and place it in a new vessel, in order to provide it nourishment for its growth. If you were Kemetic royalty, your body would be mummified and the soul capture and placed back inside. If you were a commoner, the Ab soul was captured and placed inside a

statue or some other artifact with holes packed with various curios.

After capturing the Ab soul and instilling it into a vessel. It could be given food and drink. Then, it was explained to the spirit what it could accomplish because it did not have a body and given tools and all the other things needed to continue its growth. By studying the contents found in the tomb of King Tutankhamen, we find that the deceased king was given boats, carts, building tools, hammers, weapons, even wings to instruct the spirit that it could travel anywhere.

The idea behind housing spirits is that if you take care of the spirit. Since, the spirit is no longer fettered by a physical body, it can assist you in your times of needs by foretelling the future, assisting in family matters, provide insight revolving difficult issues, aid in crop growth, protect against enemies, etc. In other words, the spirit would actively assist in all family matters, hence the term "familiar spirit."

This tradition of housing spirits has been used in Africa for ages. In the Old Kongo, spirits were housed in numerous statues called nkisi nfuiri. In the Afro-Cuban religion, Palo Mayombe religion, the spirits are housed in iron cauldrons combined with various curios. This allowed many in the Caribbean and South America to syncretize and conceal their beliefs and practices in plain sight. However, the Africans taken to North America were not so lucky.

The Africans taken to North America were stripped of everything except for the memories that resided in their heads. Then, before they could come together and build a foundation for their spiritual beliefs, Anglo slave owners would separate them from their families by selling them to other owners across the country. Fortunately, despite these horrific conditions, our ancestors did not give up. With the fragmented memories that they had within their minds, they remembered how to invoke the spirits of nature and how to make homes for their familiar spirits by housing them in small bags known as mojos, tobies or hands; boxes, dolls and buckets. They "conjured" these "familiar" spirits and named them like how their ancient ancestors in Kemet and the Kongo, like Uncle, which is believed to be a corruption of the term Nkisi.

What are Guardian Spirits?

There are many theories as to who and what the guardian spirits are. For theory suggests that the gods, goddess, angels, saints, etc. are all entities, familiar spirits, or guardian spirits known collectively as thought-forms. Thought-forms are basically blind forces that human beings create consciously but usually unconsciously with their thoughts. Whenever we take specific thoughts and emotions and identify them with things like names, symbolic attributes, etc. we are crafting our thoughts. Entities are formed from the collective unconsciousness. When we specifically identify, and give a certain type of energy human attributes, we are separating that energy from the collective unconsciousness and creating a new being. This new being is still interconnected with the collective unconscious, as we all are but it is a distinct being created out of energy, and over time becomes known as a god, goddess, saint, angel, faery, etc.

Usually the ignorant and uninformed call guardian spirits gods and goddesses whenever they see a statue or figurine but technically these images are focusing points. Images have been used as focusing points to aid in communication with spirits for ages. In fact, Christians have been using images for focal points since its inception. To this day, Christians can be found praying to Jesus, Mary, the Saints, Angels, etc. using crosses, altars, paintings, statues, etc., which is the reason the Kongolese taking to the Caribbean and South America had little trouble syncretizing their beliefs and practices.

Another theory is that the guardian angels are a personification of all our emotions that exists within us and outside of us. From this perspective, it is easy to see guardian angels as archetypes. For instance, when you see an injustice that infuriates you. It is not you who is becoming angry but your Hru Aakhuti who is reacting.

I personally think that the guardian angels are mixture of both theories and at the same time, one of those phenomena that cannot be appropriately defined or explained by science or metaphysics. When we are able to properly define, and explain a thing, we are able to control it and I do not think. We will ever be able to fully control the guardian spirits, which is how they remain a mystery. It is sort of like defining and explaining who the Creator is. We can find evidence that the Creator exist but how that evidence is understood depends upon the observer, hence making God a mystery.

You are free to believe what you want regarding the guardian spirits. However, remember that your maa (truth) is not based upon if two or more people accept your belief or not, but if your belief yields a physical result. That being said, as I said, I personally believe that the guardian spirits as a mixture between being an archetype and thought form influenced by history, thus making them elevated ancestors.

Some of these spirits are so old that their history has been lost in the sands of time and all that is remembered are their legends. However, we do know that most of the powerful spirits were per legend heroic people in life. They mastered a particular energy or force found in nature and when these people died, over time due to their influence. They crossed family boundaries and began to be honored by people outside of the family. As time, progressed, these spirits were honored by their family and other people in the community, and eventually people outside of the community. The more people honored them, the more powerful they became until eventually whole nations were honoring them from all over the world, once upon a time.

This is how the biblical Enoch became Metatron and all netcharu, loas, orishas, angels, etc. have a similar myth as to how they became gods and goddesses. In fact, per Kemetic history, it was the Kemetic King Menes who became the first guardian spirit or netchar we know as Osar (Osiris). It should be noted that Osar is not the name of a person. The actual king was named Menes or Narmer, who is an ancestral spirit. The energy that Menes (Narmer) used to unify the Kemetic people based upon ethics, morals and brought prosperity is what the Kemetic people called Osar. It can be said that King Menes studied this aspect of nature and used it to unify the people. Therefore, Osar is not a god or goddess but an energy that can exists within us and can be found in nature like thought forms.

How are Guardian Spirits Different from Spirit Guides?

Remember, spirit guides are ancestral spirit and/or spirits that are not related to you who are assigned to assist you. Guardian spirits are ancestral spirits that anyone can evoke and invoke because they are pure essences, which is the reason psychologically speaking. The closest term for this class of spirits is archetypes but, the guardian spirits are much more than that and cannot be reduced to an actual mental construct.

Another way to think about guardian spirits and spirit guides is to think of church. Most churches have a thought form that influences the congregation that attends. When you go into a church, you are exposed to that thought form, which gives you a sense or feeling of spirituality. This feeling is the church's guardian spirit. In fact, all the holy sites around the world and even many haunted areas are overseen by a guardian spirit. The spirit guides of the church are all those souls who lived and died that attend the church. The souls of these people continued to exist and if asked can assist those who attend the church. These guardian spirits are called in the Kemetic language netchars or netcharu.

As you can imagine, archeologists, historians and theologians called the Kemetic netcharu gods and goddesses because 1) they were unfamiliar with metaphysics, 2) unfamiliar with traditional African thinking and spiritual practices, and. 3) It was a serious attempt to demonize the Kemetic (and all African derived traditions) to prevent the world from knowing that the first monotheistic religion was practiced by the Kemetic people hundreds of years before the birth of Akhenaten.

So, the netchars or netcharu are thought to be like unifying energies that the souls of people with similar energy gravitates towards. Therefore, there is a netchar for protection, netchar for wealth, netchar for health, etc. In Kamta, the netcharu can be captured and harnessed by simply collecting various items associated with it. For instance, plants, herbs, stones, earth from various places, sigils, etc. can be gathered together and used to represent this energy. When these items are gathered together, they are called a het netchar, which houses the force that can be evoked or invoked.

I am aware that there are many who warn against invoking, evoking or "conjuring" but it should be understood by now that most of these warnings are based solely upon ignorant superstitions. Most of these warnings were created by people afraid of death, while others were created to discourage people from developing their magical abilities, so that they are slaves to a religion.

The fact that you have made this far is proof that you want to take charge of your life. It is also proof that your aakhu are with you and are assisting you. If it is suggested that you give them an offering for their assistance if you have a het aakhu. If not, it is highly recommended that you erect one because in order to proceed any further, you will need their assistance.

Who Are the Kemetic Guardian Spirits?

Since there are no texts that explain who and where the netcharu came from, the netcharu can be whatever you want them to be in order to support your spiritual practice. To me, understanding that the guardian spirits are energies that spirit guides gravitate towards, has led me to believe that the Kemetic guardian spirit or netcharu were the first ancient Kemetic clan or tribal leaders. As I mentioned above, per Kemetic history the first ruler to unite Kemet was King Menes or Narmer, who was later immortalized as Osar. It is my belief that Osar is the actual name of the tribe, not the ancestor Menes or Narmer. This would mean that all the names of the netchar are tribal names and not names of people. Archeologists and historians believe that the followers of a netchar were called shemsu but, I am of the mindset that these followers were clan members. In other words, there were shemsu Osar, shemsu Djahuti, shemsu Oset, and so on. This would explain why the Kemetic people described certain groups like the Hyksos as Set or being followers of Set (shemsu Set). It is not that these people worshipped Set as think in the religious sense, but Set was the name of their totem spirit or their primary guardian spirit.

From this perspective, if we assume that all the so-called major deities are the names of the major tribes, who later became the nine major netcharu who fought against Set. Therefore, the number nine (9) is an auspicious number, while the number ten (10) as seen as an inauspicious number that signifies Set (e.g. 10 is 1 separated from the whole 0), hence the 9:1 ratio.

Metaphysically speaking, the number nine is also used to represent the 9 spiritual dimensions versus the 1 physical dimension. KAMTA is believed to be more powerful than TASETT, because if each of the netcharu represent 10% of spiritual reality. Then it is composed of 90% versus TASETT, which is composed of just 10% spiritual reality. This means that the netcharu like Osar can draw upon 90% of spiritual power versus Set who draws upon 10% physical power. This 90% of spiritual power is imagined as being the collective unconscious or Superconscious, while the 10% represents the subconscious part of our being. This is the reason KAMTA is described as a fertile region, an endless ocean, the vast universe, the land of the spirits, etc., while TASETT is described as a dry and arid desert, the limited physical realm, the land of the living, etc.

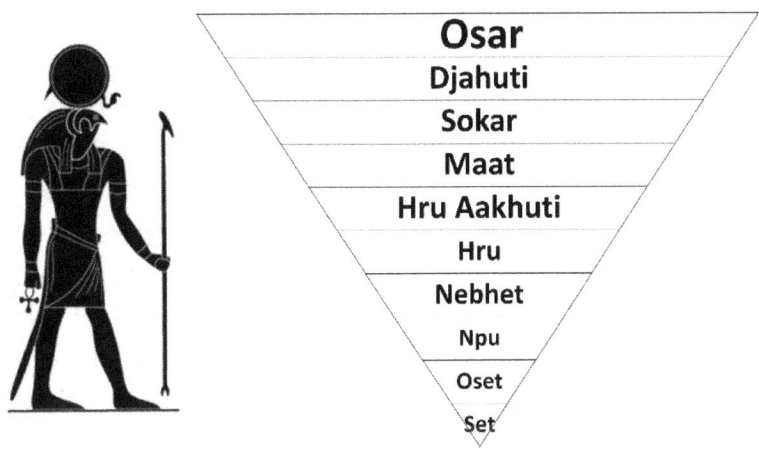

Another way of think of this is in terms of Rau Power, which is similar to the spheres of the Kabalistic Tree of Life. Remember that there is only one Rau force and both High Rau (Spiritual Light) and Lower Rau (Lesser Spiritual Light or Darkness) comes from the Rau, who is the source. Therefore, the farther one moves away from the Rau, the less Rau they have and the more earthbound they become. Understand, earthbound does not just mean that a spirit is trapped on the earth. It also refers to the fact that one is totally dependent upon their basic subconscious instincts, hence they are selfish, materialistic, egotistical, etc., which is symbolized as Set. Therefore, Osar is less earthbound because he has more Rau power versus Set who has a limited amount of Rau force.

Note, it is important that you do not err in believing that one netchar is more powerful than another because of their rank. For instance, do not err in believing that because Npu is lower than Osar in rank that Npu's influence is minimal. Without Npu, it is difficult to even approach any of the netcharu because Npu is transforms the Rau power so that it conforms to our beliefs. It is important to understand that theoretical psycho-babble is necessary for most of us to better understand who the netcharu are and how they function in our life. In other words, it is a theory of how nature or Netchar functions but Netchar (Nature) does not always to our theories. Remember, per the law of aerodynamics, birds should not be able to fly. It is best to simply accept that Osar is always at the top because he has more Spiritual Light, while Set is always at the bottom because he has less Spiritual Light. Below is a general description of the major Kemetic netcharu:

Npu (Enpu, Anubis)

Although Osar is the king of KAMTA, everything always begins with Npu. The reason is because ever since canines were domesticated, they have held a special place in the heart of human beings. Before Osar became the Lord of the Underworld, it was believed that the dead like sheep would roam aimlessly, so dogs were used corral the dead (like sheep) and prevent them from wandering into danger. This is how Npu became known as the Guide of the Dead. As a result, he is believed to provide the same protection for the curios and naïve living. Dogs also have the ability to protect us by warning us of danger. Some dogs will even fight and take on an attacker and they are also excellent hunters.

Other animals like rabbits, rats, squirrels, possums, etc. reflects Npu's witty nature. Some animals like crocodiles use wit to give the impression that they are not paying attention or are logs, which gives a hint to Npu's tricky nature. For these reasons and more, Npu (and his manifestations) are the common theme in folklore around the planet. Npu can appear as curious and mischievous child or a wise and funny elder. There is no telling, but when he appears you will know.

For instance, I have woken up exactly at 3:33 in the morning, to make sure that the doors are locked, which let me know that Npu is on guard. I have come a screeching stop while driving because three feral dogs decided to cross diagonally in a crossroad. When no other netchar will respond to your petition, Npu will.

Npu is the patron of salesmen and women, teachers, writers, communicators, orators, poets, preachers, doormen, traders, etc. He can be found everywhere there is a corner and/or crossroad, which is why he is so popular and indispensable. Figuratively and literally, nothing can be done without Npu on your side.

Purpose: Provides opportunities, opens ways for communication, to remove obstacles, general guidance, luck and protection, and finds lost things.
Colors: Red and black, red, black and white, red, black and yellow
Sacred Number: 3 and its multiples e.g. 9, 21 (2+1=3), 33, etc.
Day of the Week: Monday because it is the start of the week, Wednesday because it corresponds to the planet Mercury and is the middle of the week (Hump Day), which is imagined were Npu can be found – in the middle of everything.
Places in Nature: All crossroads, doorways (especially front doors), and entrances (including entrances into towns)
Planet or Star: Dog Star Sirius and the planet Mercury
Totem Animals: all canines such as dogs (especially feral dogs), foxes, wolves, coyotes and dingoes; rabbits, squirrels, mice, rats, monkeys, crocodiles and other animals that use wit to survive.
Sacred Objects: Crosses, crucifixes, keys (especially skeleton keys), crooked branches, staffs, canes, daggers, skulls (represent the spirits of the dead), and earth from banks, earth from crossroads, and earth from front and back doors.
Identified or Syncretized: Moses, Nine de Atocha, the apostle (or saint) Peter, Ganesha. Hermes
Preferred Offerings: Candy, popcorn, corn on the cob, chicken nuggets, cigars, rum, whiskey, coffee, small toys, objects that are red and black.

As with all of the netcharu, the more you work with your Npus the larger his het will grow because he will ask that additional items to be offered. No one really knows what spirits use these items for but for whatever reason. It is to assist you.

Osar (Asar, Ausar, Osiris)

Purpose: Peace in Home, prosperity, luck, good Fortune. Osar is also the guardian or the ruler of the entire spiritual dimension, hence his title Lord of the Underworld.

As the Lord of the Underworld, Osar is also depicted in all-black, which of course is reference to KAMTA describing that he is netchar that governs the fertile physical and spiritual grounds.

Colors: White, white/silver, all black and gold (when encompassing all KAMTA)
Number: 1
Day of the Week: Every day.
Places in Nature: Clouds, mountains, underground. Osar is the foundation of everything in Kemetic thinking. Therefore, he lies underground, so avalanches and earthquakes are seen as attempts made by Set to usurp him.
Planet or Star: Sirius, New Moon
Totem Animals: all white animals, doves, sheep, elephants, snails
Sacred Objects: All white objects, bones (especially resembling the spinal column), cotton, mummy, white stones and white linen, earth from mountains.
Identified or Syncretized: Our Lady of Mercy, Jesus (because he represents the orderly use of power and an enlightened consciousness due to rebirth).

Preferred Offerings: All white objects including white eggs, cocoa butter, shea butter, white flowers, water, coconut milk, coconut meat, white rice, pound cake, boiled yucca, potatoes, water. Never offer alcohol to Osar.

Djahuti

Purpose: Djahuti is the trusted vizier and friend of Osar. He is the archetype of wisdom and always appears as the voice of reason that leads us to making a wise and informed decision. Djahuti can be very reclusive at times but also is fond of interacting with others. He can be seen in people and things who are fond of looking at events from different perspectives. This is the reason cranes, storks, ibis are his favorite totems.

Djahuti can be found anywhere that requires wise and sagely advices, thus making him the patron of high judges.
Colors: Royal blue and white
Sacred Number: 8
Day of the Week: Thursday
Places in Nature: high courts, caves, streams, sacred mounds
Planet or Star: Jupiter (Major)
Totem Animals: owls, cranes, storks, ibis, baboons, turtles
Sacred Objects: all oracles, blank sheets of paper and scribe equipment like quills, tools for scrying.
Identified or Syncretized: King Solomon
Preferred Offerings: He accepts the same gifts as Osar.

Sokar

Purpose: Sokar is the Lord of the Cemetery and Disease. He is called upon whenever one wants assistance in healing or needs assistance in fulfilling a task that requires hard work for a long period. Unlike Hru Aakhuti who does hard work fast, Sokar is in it for the long-haul. For this reason, many say that Sokar is really an elderly feminine energy, to be precise a postmenopausal feminine energy, thus making Sokar cold and about taking care of what matters most.

Sokar is the patron of cemetery workers, mortuary workers, and miners, repair personnel (e.g. telephone, cable, plumbers, and all who work underground to ensure basic services are maintained).

Colors: His colors are indigo and black but because of his prowess he is honored with white, brown or purples.
Sacred Number: 13 and 17
Day of the Week: Saturday (Saturn-day)
Places in Nature: Cemeteries, abandoned cemeteries, the morgue, funeral homes, swamps, mortuaries, some say nursing homes are Sokar's more uplifted places of nature.
Planet or Star: Saturn
Totem Animals: owls, vultures and old birds of prey, tortoises
Sacred Objects: earth from cemeteries.

Identified or Syncretized: He is associated with the biblical Job and the parable Lazarus. I have also found him to be identified with Saint Alex (Alexis or San Alejo).
Preferred Offerings: Sokar is fond of rum, dark ales, cigars, dry white wines, sesame seeds, grains, legumes, dates and raisins.

Maat

Purpose: Maat is sometimes said to be the sister or wife of Djahuti, that helps us to accept and understand the wisdom of Djahuti. Other times she is said to be the wife of Hru Aakhuti, who prevents the warrior spirit from going too far in dispensing justice. Maat is the guardian spirit of love but this is not intimate or sexual love, but divine love and mercy that sees everyone and everything as one. Maat is about placing the needs of the many over the selfish few, which is why she is the protector of Nature and the ecosystem is under her domain.

Maat can be seen in those who are in the position to exhibit mercy like judges, attorneys, law enforcement and even the police.

Since Maat is always watching nature, she is also able to see the various cycles (ups and downs) in various systems especially the economic system. Consequently, she is also seen as a major netchar for wealth and the patron of economist and financial advisors.

Colors: Sky blue, light blue and yellow.
Sacred Number: 2 and 4
Day of the Week: Thursday the Day of Jupiter (the Minor)
Places in Nature: courthouses, mounds, sacred mounds, hills, forests that sit on the edge of towns

Planet or Star: Jupiter
Totem Animals: ostriches,
Sacred Objects: ostrich feathers, handcuffs, pistols, earth from banks, and earth from courthouses.

Identified or Syncretized: John the Baptist the last protector of the Old Testament. She also tends to work very close with indigenous cultures like the Folsom people, the Native Americans (e.g. Seminoles, Arawak, Tainos and Caribes in the Caribbean, and the various indigenous tribes in the Americas).
Preferred Offerings: Maat loves rustic foods but she also enjoys fruits, nuts, corn, rum and water.

Hru Aakhuti

Purpose: Protection from enemies, surgery, employment and anything requiring real hard work for fast results. Hru Aakhuti is not the guardian spirit of war. He does not start the war but works hard as hell to end it by any means. Hru Aakhuti can be seen in the military but also, he is the patron of surgeons, construction workers, metal workers, stockbrokers, fisherman, dock workers, professional athletes, etc. Hru Aakhuti is also the patron of entrepreneurs and if you are seriously interested in being an entrepreneur should watch the drama/history film *The Founder* to get an idea how Hru Aakhuti is in regard to business.

Colors: Blood red and/or purple
Sacred Number: 3, 4, 7 and 11
Day of the Week: Tuesday
Places in Nature: Battlefield, workplaces, fields, deep forests, construction sites, foundries, railroad crossings, docks, next to the front door next to Npu.
Planet or Star: Mars
Totem Animals: Eagles, falcons, mountain lions, bears, wolverines
Sacred Objects: machetes, all tools, all weapons, all iron objects, knives, earth from railroads, earth from battlefields, iron ore, etc.

Identified or Syncretized: Saint Peter, Archangel Michael, Saint George,

Preferred Offerings: roasted root vegetables, wild game meat, corn, chili, jerky, nuts, kidney beans, black beans and all foods favored by cowboys and hunters.

Hru

Purpose: Hru is the true heir to the throne of Osar and the lord of justice, power, victory over enemies and sensuality. Hru is the epitome of manliness and power, which is the reason he is symbolized as a lightning bolt. He is called upon whenever someone wants justice and feels as if they are being abused and taken advantage of, and when we need assistance in being justice, fair and honorable.

Hru can be seen everywhere there is position of authority and power. He is the patron of kings, rulers, managers, presidents, supervisors, etc. Most Hru can mesmerize people with their speech, which is believed to be a talent they may have picked up when growing up with their stepbrother Npu. Whatever the case, Hru are very good salespeople and keen strategists that have a knack for getting their way. This is the reason when Hru has been blinded, he becomes Set, a tyrant and dictator like Hitler.

Hru can also be found in other areas that require his scrutiny such as in chemistry and the pharmaceuticals. Hru is also very athletic and artistic, which is the reason he can be found among entertainers and professional athletes that exhibit charm and charisma, (e.g. Denzel Washington, Will Smith, George Clooney, etc.) compared to other actors.

The thing to remember about Hru is that wherever there is a place of power. Hru is usually there, which is the reason you will find him in engaged in occult and esoteric sciences.

Colors: Red and white, and sometimes gold.
Sacred Number: 6
Day of the Week: Sunday
Places in Nature: top of trees, all high places, fireplace, business desk
Planet or Star: Sun
Totem Animals: Hawks, rams, bulls, lions, roosters, goats, horses
Sacred Objects: scepters, crowns, axes, hammers, wood staffs, swords, sledge hammers
Identified or Syncretized: Saint Gerome, Santa Barbara, Zeus the Lightning Thrower
Preferred Offerings: red apples, okra, plantains, bananas, almonds, corn, peppers, spicy foods, occasionally cigars and tobacco, red wine, ale, stouts, liquor

Nebhet

Purpose: Nebhet is netchar love. Therefore, art, beauty, diplomacy, fertility, intimacy, marriage, sex, relationships, and money fall under her domain.

She is one of the most famous netchar because Nebhet loves things that shine and glimmer. She can be seen all throughout the entertainment industry as she is the patron of actors/actresses, filmmakers, singers, and TV personalities. She is found in the beauty and cosmetic industry and wherever there is sweet smelling fragrances. She is also the patron of cooks and chefs. Nebhet works well with other fertility and household spirits like the dwarf netchar Bes.

Colors: Yellow (and/or gold), green, pink and coral
Sacred Number: 5
Day of the Week: Friday
Places in Nature: Parks, river shores, botanical gardens, kitchen and master bedroom
Planet or Star: Venus, new crescent moon
Totem Animals: Peacocks, cats, female big cats, ducks, pheasants and parrots
Sacred Objects: jewelry, bells, mirrors, combs and seashells
Identified or Syncretized: Oshun, Lady of Caridad del Cobre, Saint Martha, Aphrodite, Venus and all energies that use beauty and sweetness to tame a wild heart.
Preferred Offerings: honey, spinach, cinnamon, mangoes, strawberries, peaches, pumpkins, oranges, passion fruits, light pastries and seafood.

Oset

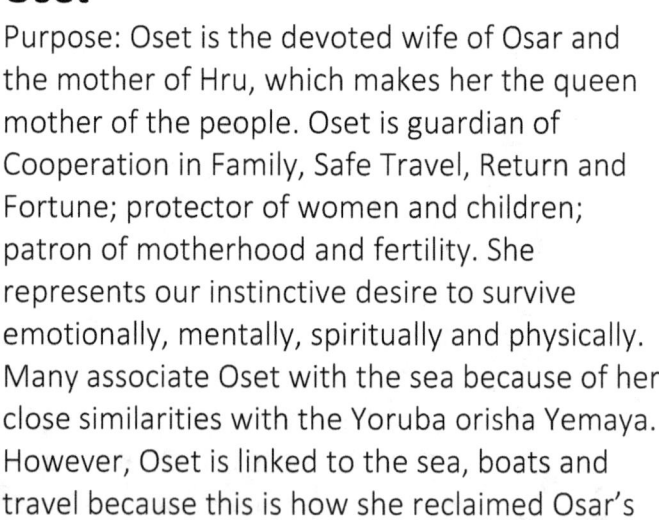

Purpose: Oset is the devoted wife of Osar and the mother of Hru, which makes her the queen mother of the people. Oset is guardian of Cooperation in Family, Safe Travel, Return and Fortune; protector of women and children; patron of motherhood and fertility. She represents our instinctive desire to survive emotionally, mentally, spiritually and physically. Many associate Oset with the sea because of her close similarities with the Yoruba orisha Yemaya. However, Oset is linked to the sea, boats and travel because this is how she reclaimed Osar's body from the foreign lands. Consequently, the veneration of Oset spread outside of Kemet and temples dedicated to her were found as far as Europe. This is because everyone loves and respects the Divine Mother, which is why the Virgin Mary was modeled after Oset.

Colors: Turquoise blue, ocean blue or blue and white.
Sacred Number: 7
Day of the Week: Monday because it is Moon Day
Places in Nature: Seas, beaches shores, places where children congregate such as the den.
Planet or Star: Moon (especially full moon)
Totem Animals: All manner of fish, shorebirds,
Sacred Objects: Throne, crescent moon, sailboats, seashells, conch shells, starfish, fishing nets, anchors,
Identified or Syncretized: Yemaya, Virgin Mary, Our Lady of Miraculous Medals,
Preferred Offerings: beer, water, watermelons, cantaloupes, pineapples, molasses, cornmeal, saltwater candy, seafood.

Lesson Four: Basic Instructions on Working with the Netcharu (Guardian Spirits)

To Create a Rapport with the Netchar

Since there are no texts that has been recovered explaining who and where the netcharu originated from. It is my belief that the original netcharu were originally ancient Kemetic clan or tribal leaders. When these tribal leaders died, they were immortalized and became immortal tribal leaders over a clan of spirits. Consequently, each netcharu is a host of spirits that have gathered in the netchar's name but is dominated by one netchar who presides over all of the spirits within that spiritual tribal clan. For instance, there is a dominant Hruaakhuti who presides over a host of Hruaakhuti spirits because there is an infinite number of Hruaakhutis. The difference between them is that my Hruaakhuti may not be the same as your Hruaakhuti, but they are the spirits of souls who once walked the earth and were warriors, fighters, hard workers, soldiers, etc.

To build a rapport with the netchar, familiarize yourself with their legend, their purpose, colors, day of the week, totems, etc. A lot of times, you will find that the netchar tried to make their presence known but you just did not know their call signs. Anyway, purchase an image of the netchar and set a candle between you and their image. Next, gaze at the netchar's in the most attentive manner. Then wait until you hear the netchar speak or sense the netchar's presence. Once you finish the practice, thank the netchar and extinguish the candle.

Another way to work with the netchar is to talk to them daily. To do this simply gaze at their image and soak in every detail. Then, imagine seeing the netchar in your mind's eye. You do not have remember the image exactly how it is but try to recall their image to mind. Once you have done this, talk to the netchar as if you would a friend or acquaintance. I try to always greet my netchar by telling them "Hetep" meaning "Peace & blessings."

You will know when the netchar is speaking with you because you will receive signs that corresponds to them. It is important to note that the netcharu do not appear the same way for everyone. Some netcharu will make a dramatic appearance, whiles others will appear subtly. For instance, I met my Npu when I was at a crossroad situation preparing to go down a road that was going to lead me down a quick and dangerous path. The interesting thing as you read in previous parts of this book, my Npu had been vying for my attention for a while, which is how I met Papa. But, all of the netcharu do not appear this way. For instance, my Hru appeared to me in a dream. I remember it like it happened last night. One night I had a dream that I was in a tribal village in what I think was Africa. There were a men and women, young and old sitting in a circle, and they were all wearing a vibrant red African attire. As I approached the group, an elder said, "Welcome Hru. You made it" as they directed me to the center of the circle. But, not all your netcharu will appear in these manners. For instance, I met my Sokar when I became ill and so on.

Working and Making Offerings to the Netchar
I have heard people say that when you talk to the netcharu that you must beg them to do things and make sure you do not renege on your offerings. Well, I think this is the case for people who worship their spirits but not for those who see them as an elevated or deified ancestor.

The same way you talk to your ancestor, I think is the same way you should talk to the netcharu. Meaning, when I have a problem, I tell the appropriate netchar what my problem is and what I want. I never tell me netcharu how to solve my problems. I just tell them what I want and leave it in their hands. Then, I go about my business. There are several ways this can be done. For instance, I may symbolize the problem as a small pebble and name the pebble after the problem. Then, tell the netchar what I want and throw the pebble behind my back, leave at the foot of a tree, at a crossroad or even on the netchar's shrine. Then, I go about my business as if I never asked for help.

Or, I may write or tell the netchar "Help me do _____" and then, act as if I never even asked for help.

When I receive a desired solution, I give an offering to the netchar in appreciation for their assistance. Occasionally, to get my netchar's to react real fast I might say, "Help me to do _____" and I will give you _____."

I know some people may be against developing a "*quid pro quo*" relationship with their spirits but remember, this is the only way human beings and spirits will appreciate and value the rapport we share. The spirits need us, just as much as we need them.

Sometimes, if you have developed a rapport with the netchar, they will work on your behalf without you asking. For instance, one day my wife and I were having a heated argument because neither one of us was seeing the other person's perspective. Then, my wife got called away for her job where she encountered a police officer. The police officer talked to my wife about a few things and one of the subjects that came up was what my wife and I were arguing about, which gave her a new perspective. When she told me, this story the next day, I knew that it was Maat looking over us, so I gave her an offering.

Of course, to work with the netcharu from this perspective you must really familiarize yourself with the netchar's numbers, totems, colors, archetypes, stories, etc. This requires a little imagination and memorization, which means you need to study them but do not force it. It is only in relax states that our BA will allow messages to enter our awareness about the netchar. So, do not intellectualize, too much will hinder the process. Just be mindful who you are working with because when the netchar makes themselves known, you will know it.

To Build a Het Netchar (Guardian Spirit House)

A Het Netchar literally means a "House for the Guardian Spirit." It is a place for the spirits associated with the netchar to reside. It is also a dwelling for those unknown and forgotten spirits to dwell and assist the netchar. This is because many of these spirits do not have loved ones who make offerings to assist them in their development. So, these spirits agree to work under the guidance of a popular netchar. In return the netchar allows the food, drink, money, etc. offered to the netchar, to be used by these spirits to assist them in their development. Basically, the netchar provides for these spirits and the spirit works for the netchar in return.

Therefore, to keep these employed, we need to build a het netchar (guardian spirit house) to house these spirits. To make a home for these spirits you can use a plant, painting, statue, talisman, rock, crystal, etc. However, if the het netchar is boring and dull looking, it will be boring and dull looking to your spirits. Therefore, the best way to ensure that this altar has qualities that will make you interact with it is by making a home for the spirits using a pot with a statue, so that it stirs your emotions of interest.

The purpose of the pot is to serve as a literal "house" for the spirit, while the statue provides the spirit with a "physical body." Most of the spirits pots can be made with painted clay pots, but some spirits like Hru Aakhuti will prefer an iron pot or cauldron.

To make the "house," there are several ways that this can be accomplished. I am providing general instructions on how this can be constructed. Feel free to add or take away per your desire. First, take a clay pot and paint it in the colors of the netcharu you want to honor. For instance, if you were making a het for Npu, you may paint the colors of the pot red on the outside and black on the inside with white trim. Simply follow your intuition.

Second, on the inside of the clay pot draw the maa aankh using chalk. Next, add items that are sacred to the netchar. (See the netchar listing above). Do not worry about having all of the items. As your relationship with the netchar evolves so will the het. Once the het is complete, consecrate it by spraying it with three mouthfuls of rum and three puffs of smoke.

Basic Ritual for the Het Netchar (Guardian Spirit House)

Besides providing a space for spirits associated with the netchar to reside, the Het Netchar basically acts like a miniature world of the netchar. For instance, instead of going to the crossroad to invoke Npu, the Npu's het netchar does not symbolize the crossroad but is a crossroad. If you wanted to evoke Osar, instead of going to a mountain or a cave. Osar's het netchar is the mountain or cave. Therefore, work done with the het netchar is for long term work because it acts as a charm. For instance, to sweeten a relationship, you could take a medicine jar and put the names of the individual inside, then cover it with honey.

1. Light a candle.
2. Then say, "Nebhet, this relationship to be sweet, etc. "
3. I might rub money between my hands and lay it on the het. Since I will not be using the money offered to the spirits of the netchar, occasionally I may burn the money so that it transforms from the physical realm to the spiritual realm quicker. I put the ashes in an ashtray.

4. Then I would say something like, "Thank you for helping me to get _____. "This statement can be chanted as many times as you like until it resonates with you.
5. Then, I place the medicine jar in the spirit's het.

As long as the jar is inside the het, Nebhet will continue to influence the relationship. Understand, that this does not mean that the couple will not have arguments but that Nebhet will keep the individuals focused on loving one another. This can be done for any long-term work.

More Hints on Offerings and Sacrifices to the Netchar

Remember, after voicing or writing your petition, it is best to make an offering or sacrifice in exchange for what you want because we as human beings have a bad habit of abusing and misusing anything that is given freely. We have been programmed from birth to be suspicious of anything receive something freely, so feel it appropriate to always earn what we receive.

Now contrary to popular belief, the netcharu will accept that is offered to them because what they want more than anything is time and energy. This is what all spirits miss and why veneration is so important. So, you can offer them anything because it is not about the offering itself, but the time and energy put into the offering. For instance, you can offer the netcharu cake or any food you think they will like. It does not matter to them. Simply let the food offering sit for the time being and when you sense that the netchar has absorbed some of the food's essence. Eat it, put it in a compost or throw it, your choice.

Personally, I do not like leaving food around the house because it attracts pests. Instead I may offer rum, beer, white candles or candles in the netchar's preferred color, as a general offering. The more elaborate the offering the more elaborate the request granted. For instance, if a netchar is petitioned for a boon like recovery from an illness, increase in salary, etc. Then, once the petition is granted, I may offer flowers, an additional item on their het, etc.

Basically, the point being made is that you can offer anything so long as you have a genuine feeling of appreciation and gratitude to the netchar for helping you. And, the best way to generate this feeling is to make a promise to give up something or sacrifices, for what you want. The best things to promise to give up or sacrifice are money and/or a bad habit you want to change. For instance, if I were to ask Nebhet to help me get something and I was offering money, like a five-dollar bill or $1 bill for five days, since Nebhet's number is five.

I offer different things for different reasons and depending on the circumstances. Some of the best offerings in my opinion are personal sacrifices. Again, if you do not live in an agricultural society or community, put the knife down. You do not need to sacrifice an animal and you shouldn't because that animal does not have the same meaning to you, as it does for people from an agricultural society. However, things you care about like a habit do have some significance. This is where fasting comes into the picture. You can fast for anything so long as it does not put your life in danger and is not done to the extreme.

For instance, you could fast for Nebhet by offering something that you really want to change, such as abstaining from consuming candy for 25 days, since 5 days x 5 days is 25. You could do this for any of the netchar, like for nine days (3 x 3) fast to Npu for him to help you increase your sales, and so on.

All you have do to is simply say that in place of the money, you make a promise to the netchar. Now, don't make a promise of something that is extremely difficult. You don't want to renege on your promise.

For instance, if you are a smoker, don't promise to give up smoking and knowing you are having difficulty accomplishing this goal. You will easily fail and renege on your promise. Try to promise something that you need to work on and can accomplish like your anger. For instance, you could say, "Nebhet, I offer you my anger for five days." This means that for the next five days you better be pleasant and sweet acting no matter what the cost. Even, when someone calls you out of your name or a driver cuts you off. Be sweet.

For the record, it is usually easier to just make a tangible offering but I am providing this information about personal promises (or sacrifice) to show how this can be accomplish with spiritual development. The spirits know that anyone can give a tangible offering, but real commitment comes from making promises. When spirits see that you are serious to the point that you are willing to make a personal promise or sacrifice. It really gets the spirit's attention because spirits are about evolution and growth.

One more thing, you can do this ritual as many times as you like because this is a tradition, not a religion. Remember traditions do not have a lot of rules except for the ones that you make up. It is religion that has a host of rules. The whole purpose of doing the ritual is to generate a positive feeling towards your goals, so if you do not feel good after doing the ritual once. Do it a few more times.

As I mentioned above, if I were working with Nebhet I might offer her a $1 bill for five consecutive days for a total of five days because this is her sacred number. I would not nag and pester her by doing the ritual excessively because besides illustrating a lack of faith, it also causes creates stress and prevents the magick from being accomplished. This is the main reason most prayers are not answered because the petitioner is obsessing over the results. Let the spirit do their job and you go about doing yours.

How to Do Constructive & Destructive Magick

I hope by now you understand that there is no such thing as good or evil. Good and evil are Western concepts that have been created based upon a limited view of our universe. Remember, what is good for one could be interpreted as being evil by another. Therefore, we cannot use ethics and morals as a ruler for living our life. We must rely upon Maa to guide and navigate us through this world of constant change.

From this perspective, it is best to think of magick as being either constructive or destructive. Constructive magick is used to build and create something you want to manifest in your life, while destructive magick is used to tear down and remove something in your life.

The reason magick is used is because shamans and other natural healers from around the world, know that there are a lot of things outside of their physical control, so they rely upon constructive magick for healing, protection, increasing business opportunities, blessings, improving family relations and for use in war. The objective is always to establish and maintain balance. The general idea to influence a situation is to name a thing after the person or thing you want to influence. For instance, one day I had a relative that was really down on their luck. They were having problems getting a job, which was causing them financial woes and strife with their spouse. This relative just needed a door opened, so after doing a reading to determine if it were okay to assist them. I took a penny and named it them, then I placed it heads up. On top of the penny, I placed a white candle and simply called upon my Npus to assist in opening this individual's way. Several days later, I got word that they got a good paying job. Afterwards, I gave my Spirits an offering to express my thanks.

It is important that sometimes destructive magick is necessary. For instance, is it fair for people to be terrorized? No and when you have explored every option to resolve a situation peacefully. Sometimes you have to use more destructive means. Again, magick can be used and sometimes in this case, I will simply take a penny, name it and turn it tails side up. Then, reverse a candle and state the problem. Again, this is giving the issue to the Spirits. Note that you can use any object you want anywhere such as a pebble, a coconut, an orange, etc. The thing to remember is that you are one performing the magick, so it does not matter what anyone else's believe. It works so long as you believe it does.

Traditional Blessings for a New Way of Life
In many traditional societies that have not been touched by Western influence, it is customary to call upon all the benevolent spirits for the blessing of a new home, blessing a new marriage, and blessing for safe travel of a loved one. Blessings can also be done for any new project. Again, there is no right or wrong way to perform this ritual. Simply 1) light sandalwood incense (and/or cigar smoke if possible) and light candles to invite the benevolent spirits. In addition, you can also offer a bowl of fruit for new beginning or liquor. Follow your intuition. 2) Pray aloud (or silently) and thank the spirits for all the blessings you have received thus far, and. 3) Tell the spirits to accept the offerings that have been given and to bless whatever.

To secure the blessings of the spirits, tie a string pertaining to the netchar on the wrist of the recipient. If this is well planned, you can instead imbue a beaded necklace or bracelet with the Spirits' blessing and give as a gift.

PART TWO:
Practicing KAMTA

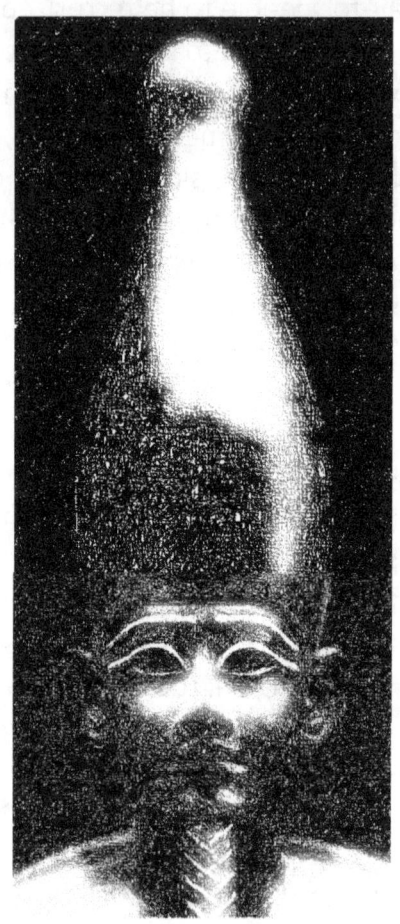

"The power of a shaman is known by their work in the world."
Rufino, Bolivian Alymara Shaman

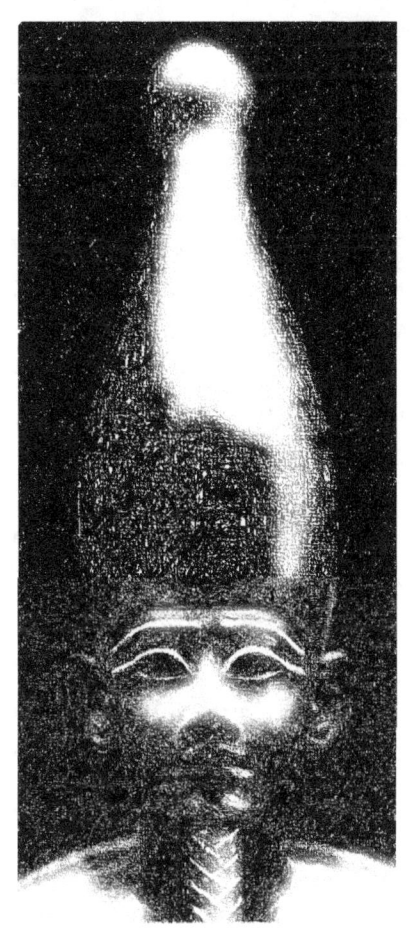

FIVE:
Why Were We Created

If we believe that our Perfect Creator is omnipotent, all-knowing and everywhere, then we must accept that nothing happens in our life accidentally or coincidentally. Everything that occurs in our life is part of a Divine Plan. This would mean that the only reason accidents and coincidences appear to exist is because of the concept we call Time.

Time creates a delay that makes it appear that every effect occurs accidentally, coincidentally and at random. But we live in Cause and Effect world, which means for every Cause there is an Effect. Hence, everything that goes up must come down, for every right there is a left, things that get hot must eventually become cool, etc. This duality is due to Maa and it is because of Maa everything in our reality must be balanced. For instance, if we threw a rock in the air. We see that it would fall back down to the earth because of Cause and Effect, or Maa. However, we fail to see how Cause and Effect of our actions and behaviors effect our lives.

Our Perfect Creator on the other hand, sees and knows everything because the Divine exists outside of the realm of Time, hence the Creator's Kemetic title Nebertcher – the Lord of All Things. This means that our Perfect Creator already knows what, when, where, why and how we are going to sin before we sin because Nebertcher is...All-Knowing. Therefore, there has to be a more profound reason why our Perfect Creator allows sin – an imperfection– to exist than the reason contemporary theologians have given us. There has to be a more profound reason why our Perfect Creator allows all of the atrocities that exists to continue to do so.

The Story of Ra & Oset

According to Kemetic creation theory, everything that exist came out of *nyun,* a great void or the primeval waters of creation, symbolized on the maa aankh as the horizontal line that separates the hidden spiritual world below from the visible physical world above.

When the Creator called Itself into existence, finding nowhere to stand caused the Maa to emerge out of the nyun. This is symbolized as the vertical line on the maa aankh.

Due to the Maa, which brought balance and duality into our world. The Perfect Creator spat out Shu and emitted Tefnut. Shu is the forceful, aggressive, upward, and hot moving energy that symbolizes the natural force of expansion, heat, light, dryness, masculinity, and activity, loudness, outward, active, firm, rational, logical, mathematical and analytical, hence the Kemetic yang. While Tefnut is the downward moving force that symbolizes the natural force of contraction, coolness, darkness, dampness, wetness, femininity, and inertia, quiet, inward, inactive, soft, and imaginative.

Shu and Tefnut like Lisa and Mawu or Yang and Yin, are said to be brother and sister or husband and wife because they are inseparable and interdependent upon one another. One cannot exist without the other because of the Maa. Therefore, Shu is also exuberance, motion, the living, sunlight, upward movement, the day, the heavens, top, head, studying, etc. and is seen in men because traditionally men were more extroverts that hunted for food and fought invaders.

While Tefnut also symbolized sadness, fatigue, selfishness, depression, religion, philosophy, depression, weakness, going within or meditation, the dead, the earth, stillness of the night, the bottom, the back, creativity, greed, sleeping, etc. Tefnut traditionally speaking was symbolized as women because women were more introverted in their activities. They stayed at home and cared for the family and children. The womb is considered to also be the sign of Tefnut as well as the receiving of the sperm.

It should be noted that Shu and Tefnut have nothing to do with chauvinism and feminism but divine concepts of Cause and Effect, which is the reason they are symbolized on the maa aankh as counter-clockwise movements that propel the sun.

Through the union of Shu and Tefnut, the ethereal Nut and the earthly Geb were created. Nut is not the so-called sky goddess but the spiritual attributes that exist in all life. Geb is the physical attributes that exist in all life. Together they created the southern region of the country known as Upper Kemet or KAMTA[3] – the Black Lands and the northern section became known as Lower Kemet or TASETT – the Red Lands. Through the union of Nut and Geb, human beings came into existence.

Before the beginning of human time, human beings like all of creation were created perfect because we were created by a Perfect Creator, but according, to legend, Oset was a determined woman who wanted to know the secret name of Ra, so that she could become a divine being that was cherished in the heavens and the earth. So Oset concocted of a plan to get Ra to share his secret name with her.

She noticed that every day, Ra who was up in age would dribble and his spit would fall upon the earth. So, she decided one day to

---

[3] When referring to the placement on the maa**Error! Bookmark not defined.** aankh, the word KAMTA is capitalized to distinguish it from the name of the tradition.

gather Ra's slobber, which fell on the ground and knead it into a serpent in the form of a spear. Once her creation was finished, she placed the serpent upright before her face, but laid it on the path so that when Ra would pass the serpent would afflict him.

As before, Ra arose and set forth upon his daily journey and when he came across the serpent lying on the path; it bit him causing the sacred fire of life to depart from him. Ra opened his mouth and cried out, "What has happened?" and all that was with him exclaimed, "What is it?" but, Ra could not answer because his members quaked, his mouth trembled because the poison of the serpent had swiftly spread throughout his body.

Ra stated to all those who had accompanied him on his journey to tell Khepera that a dire calamity had fallen upon him, thereby preventing him from continuing his journey. He exclaimed that he didn't see what ailed him or what caused the great pain and agony that he was in, nor did he know who had did it to him. All that he knew was that he had never felt pain like the pain that he was in. Ra in total disbelief that someone would dare harm him cried out that he was a prince, the son of a prince, a sacred essence that came from God. Ra cried out further that he was the son of a great one whose name was planned and as a result, he had a multitude of names and a multitude of forms and he exists in everything.

Ra further proclaimed that all heralds his coming as his father and mother utter his name, that was secret and hidden within him by the one that begat him, which he would not divulge to anyone for fear that they would have dominion over him. Ra recounted his journey by stating that he came forth to survey all that he created and it was while passing through the world that something mysteriously stung him. "What was that?" Ra wondered. Was it fire that made him hotter than fire or water that made him feel so cold, he wondered that made his heart feel like it was on fire, his body tremble and flesh to shake with sweat.

Furious, Ra called upon all of his children to come before him and to assist him in destroying the illness, but none could heal Ra and wept heavily. When Oset appeared before the trembling king, she asked Ra, what had happened to him and was it a serpent that rose against him and bit him. She told Ra that with his power and her words she could drive the illness away.

Ra told Oset, that he was passing along my daily journey, and I was going through the two regions of my lands according to my heart's desire. In order to see that which he had created, when suddenly out of nowhere! A serpent bit him, which he did not see. Ra asked was it fire or was it water because he was colder than water and hotter than fire. Ra said that his flesh sweat, quaked, and his eyes have no strength. He told Oset that he could not even see the sky and that sweat rushed to his face as if he was in the summer.

Oset told the great Ra that she would drive the poison of the serpent away only if he would tell her his secret name, because whosoever shall be delivered by his secret name would live.

Ra responded telling Oset that "*I have made the heavens and the earth, I have ordered the mountains, I have created all that is above them, I have made the water, I have made to come into being the great and wide sea, I have made the 'Bull of his mother,' from whom spring the delights of love. I have made the heavens, I have stretched out the two horizons like a curtain, and I have placed the soul of the gods within them. I am he who, if he openeth his eyes, doth make the light, and, if he closeth them, darkness cometh into being. At his command the Nile riseth, and the gods know not his name. I have made the hours, I have created the days, I bring forward the festivals of the year, and I created the Nile-flood. I make the fire of life, and I provide food in the houses. I am Khepera in the morning, I am Ra at noon, and I am Tmu at evening."*

The poison burned through Ra's body and prevented the great one from walking. Oset noticing that Ra's condition was getting worse told him that what he has said is not his hidden name and it is not driving the poison away. Again, she asked that Ra reveal his secret name to her as the poison burned deeper and hotter in Ra's body.

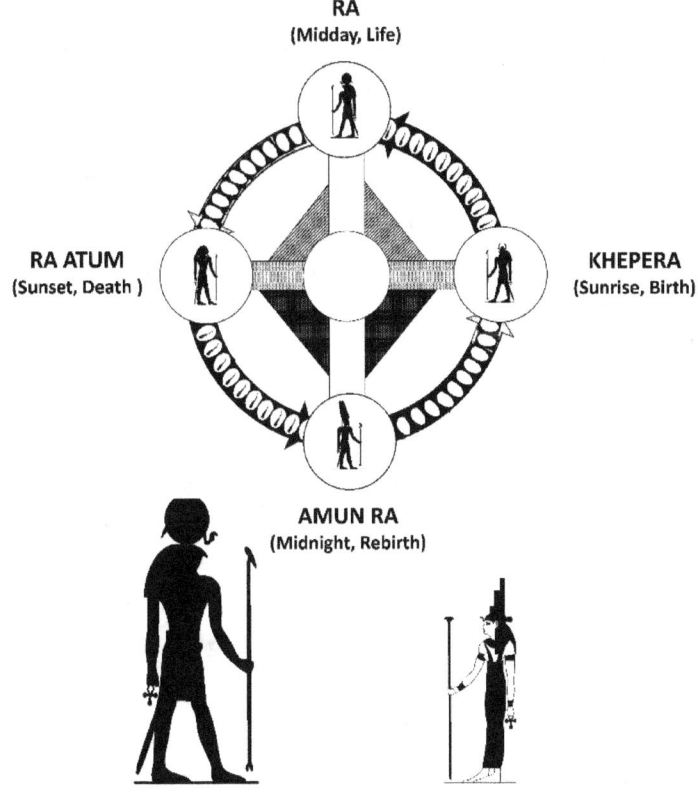

Finally, Ra complied and hid himself from the company before him and when the two could not be seen the name of Ra passed from his body into her. And when the heart of Ra came forth, Oset called her son Hru to come forth saying, "Ra hath bound himself by an oath to deliver up his two eyes" (i.e., the sun and moon). After Oset took the name of Ra she drove the poison out of Ra's body and commanded the Eye of Hru to go forth and shine outside of Ra's mouth.

She enchanted "May Ra live and the poison die and the poison die and Ra live". And, that is how the great Ra who suffered the frailty and weakness of a man almost perished but was healed.

The Truth of the Story of Ra & Oset

The purpose of the *Story of Ra and Oset* is to give some explanation as to why human beings have problems in our life. To understand the truth of the Story we have to accept that Ra, as mentioned earlier, is not aten (the sun or the so-called sun-god), but is the symbol of God's Power, and. Oset, is the symbol of human desire. This means that according to the Kemetic sages, the reason Oset tricked Ra in the first place is because she wanted fulfillment.

To understand what fulfillment means imagine you are a player on a little league basketball team and there is a big game coming up. The coach promises your team that if your team wins the game, he will reward you all with pizza. So, you practice dribbling and shooting the ball because you want to do your part to help your team win. Then, on the day of the big game, you guys play an amazing game and wins.

As you and your teammates are high-fiving each other. You notice out of the corner of your eye, that your coach is giving the other team's coach money because they made a deal, to buy the opposing team pizza if they purposely loss. Apparently, the coach knew your team would try hard but did not believe that your team could win. So, he paid the other team off in order to keep from hurting your teams' feelings.

How would you feel about this? Do you feel as if you deserve the pizza? Do you feel that your team was great? Would you want a chance to prove that your team was better? Do you feel like you earned the reward?

Most of us would feel really salty because the game was given to us. In other words, we did not really win. It did not matter that we were given a reward (pizza in this case), the fact of the matter is that most of us would feel bad because we did not earn the win. Whenever we as human beings do not earn what we want. Most of the time, we do not appreciate it. In fact, historically we take anything and everything given to us freely for granted and we waste it.

For instance, if you give a child everything that they want. The child grows up to be a spoiled entitled brat. History has shown us time and time again, that when individuals receive large sums of that they did not earn. They squander it and we have numerous artists, actors, entertainers and athletes to verify this.

Why do we do we behave in this manner?

According to psychologist Abraham Maslow (1908 – 1970), who studied the lives of Albert, Einstein, Eleanor Roosevelt, Frederick Douglass and many other exemplary individuals, it is because we all have a need for self-fulfillment. In Maslow's *Hierarchy of Needs,* Maslow theorizes that we each have five types of desires that make us happy. These desires or needs from the lowest to the highest degree of intensity are:

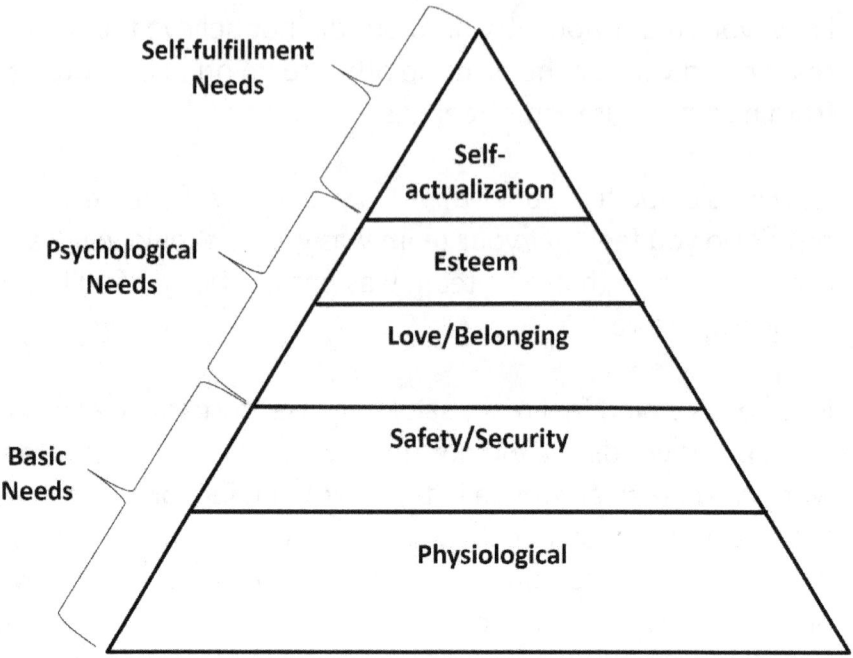

Physiological: breathing, food, water, shelter, sex, sleep, homeostasis, excretion, warmth.

Safety: security of body: employment, resources, morality, the family, health, property, assets.

Love/Belonging: family, friendship, sexual intimacy, sense of belonging.

Esteem: self-esteem, confidence, achievement, respect of others, respect by others, self-worth, and.

Self-actualization: achieving one's full potential, including creativity, spontaneity, problem solving, lack of prejudice, acceptance of facts, inner fulfilment, etc.

The need for food, water, sex and safety are our **Basic Needs** that human beings and animals both desires.

The need to belong to a group (family, friends, community, etc.) as well as the desire for honor, power and wealth are all human desires or **Psychological Needs** that can only be obtain by interacting with other human beings.

However, **Self-fulfillment Needs** goes beyond mere human capabilities and into the spiritual dimension. This desire creates an inherent need to search for the purpose of life, and because it is a spiritual desire. This need cannot be satisfied physically. This is the reason when a person reaches this desire; no amount of money, honor, knowledge, power, etc. will satisfy them. The only way to satisfy this desire is through spirituality, hence the term Amun Ra (the Hidden Name of Ra). The term Hidden is a code word signifying something that is beyond our physical sight. In other words, it is immaterial (spiritual).

Many people think that spirituality is all about chanting, meditating, praying and ascetic living (abstaining, fasting, self-abnegating, a lot of self-denying, self-discipline, etc.) requiring that one become a monk or a pupil of a guru who sits at their feet on top of a mountain. But these are all techniques (abstaining, fasting, self-abnegating, a lot of self-denying, self-discipline, etc.) related to attaining self-fulfillment. It is not spirituality per se. The main purpose of spirituality is to become a god or goddess. To be more specific:

- To control our own fate,
- To achieve anything at will,
- To be the creator of our own happiness, and.
- To share our contentment, success and gratification with others.

In other words, the reason Oset tricked Ra into revealing his "Hidden" name was because she had everything. Our Perfect Creator created Ra so that everything that was created was Perfect. Remember, our Perfect Creator is Perfect, so God cannot make a mistake, which means Oset (we) had everything she ever wanted except but it was too Perfect.

Imagine every time you do something it turns out perfect with no opposition. Boring, right? It also breeds complacency but if we must earn what we want by working hard. Now we have a bit of drama that we do not mind engaging in because we have a reward to look forward to. When we earn something, no one can take what we have earned away from us. Yes, it is going to be a struggle but since we are made in the image of the Divine. Everything we do is still going to work out for the best.

Oset tricked Rau because she wanted to control her own fate.

Oset did not want to be told that she is great because she is made in the likeness of the Perfect Creator. She wanted to prove it to herself. She wanted to know without a shadow of doubt that she is a divine for being. She wanted to create and be the source of her own happiness.

To fulfill her desire, Ra (at the Ra moment) created opposition for Oset, so that she would have to earn true fulfillment by striving to get to Amun Ra. In other words, to get to the true Source – Amun Ra – she had to earn her way by going within.

Oset became legendary throughout Kemet and the ancient world because she opened the way. For humanity to transcend his or her animalistic nature and tap into the BA – the Divine Spark. Simply put, Oset opened the way for us to become gods and goddesses by putting our salvation in our own hands, so we do not have to wait for God to save us.

This truth should resonate strongly with people who have overcome illnesses, addictions, extreme problematic situations, etc. It should also make sense why people abstain, fast, self-abnegate, deny themselves pleasures, self-discipline, etc. If you are familiar with traditional spiritual systems from the mystic path, it should also make sense now why these techniques are related to inner vision, intuition, visions, etc.

We hear people say it all the time. Suddenly, "It hit me." or something strange and mysterious happened. The next thing you know they had a change of heart. They loss the desire to live a certain way. They did a complete 360-degree change. All of this is because of looking for someone to save them. They went within into Amun Ra and saved themselves. By going within, they conceived a solution to resolve their own problems.

Now, returning to our little league basketball team, when we play the opposing team this time. Win or lose, they want a sense of accomplishment. If the team loses, they will be disappointed but they will try harder so that we can beat them the next time until they win. Trying harder requires to some degree abstaining, fasting, self-abnegating, a lot of self-denying, etc. to get to the Amun Ra moment. It is denying yourself the immediate gratification of the physical, in order to tap into the spiritual. This is the reason Amun Ra rests on the other side in KAMTA. We will also see shortly, that this is the reason Osar rests under Amun Ra within KAMTA and presides over agriculture and everything underground. It is a metaphorical reminder to stop seeking for inclusion as is done by African American actors/actresses in Hollywood, and tap into the Divine power, and make your own.

Lesson Five: Discovering Your Purpose

Identifying Patterns
The purpose of this exercise is to identify the problem areas that exist in your life. Using the information from the previous exercise you should have noted a familiar pattern that arises. Do you find yourself struggling to get a mate? To keep a job. To keep bills paid. To keep a peaceful home. Etc.? Whatever you struggle with, whatever problems you have, etc. write them down and observe how dealt with these issues. Note that although it is a Western cultural practice to try and avoid every problem that we encounter and shift blame to everything that goes wrong in our life. It is not wise to do because the problem does not go away. The time has come to realize that the problem you are running away is the reason you are here.

Therefore, write a list of reoccurring problems that you struggle with. By writing them down, you are able to make a mental note when they appear and understand that this has to do with your destiny.

Receiving Fulfillment from Amun Ra
Have you ever noticed how easy it is to do the wrong thing versus doing what is right? I mean, a person cusses you out for no reason, and the thought that goes through your mind is to reach out and hit them. It is not the right thing to do but it is the easiest thing.

Why should you resist doing what is easy?

Why should you not hit them?

It is because when you do what is easy you do what is natural, which invokes the power of Ra. The Ra moment you will recall deals with physical prowess and aggression. In the future you will see that this moment corresponds to Set, our main foe spirit.

However, when you do what is right, you invoke the supernatural power of Amun Ra. The Amun Ra moment deals with spiritual prowess and it corresponds to Osar, our main guardian spirits as well as all of the other benevolent spiritual forces, hence the 90%.

As you can see, this has nothing to do with ethics and morals. It is all about power. Doing what is Right is about accessing spiritual power.

Doing what is Easy is doing what is natural, while doing what is Right is doing is Supernatural.

When we do what is Right, it is going against our physical nature (sahu) and tenses our spiritual muscles (BA). The more we do what is Right by being proactive, the stronger spiritually we become because we are relying upon the higher part of our being (our BA), which is connected to Amun Ra. This is how we get true fulfillment. The reason Oset tricked Ra and why she (the Virgin Mary[4] as well) was so famous in the ancient world, is because her rouse allowed us to get fulfillment.

Therefore, whenever there is an obstacle that appears, by resisting reacting to it the way we normally would. We tap into this Hidden Power.

Fulfillment comes Amun Ra in the following manner:

1. *A Difficulty Occurs.*
   You are waiting for someone to exit out of a parking space,

---

[4] The early Christian writers tried to superimpose Oset onto the Virgin Mary by saying that she gave all people access to Jesus.

and as soon as you leave. Another driver rushes in and takes the parking space you were waiting for.

2. **Naturally you want to react.**
It is natural for you to react by becoming angry and cussing out of the driver out. Resist the urge and realize that this behavior does not generate supernatural power.

3. **Resist the Urge to React.**
Instead of going after the driver or cussing the driver out. Do the exact opposite. Smile, laugh, etc. Do not give into your natural emotions. Remember, it is not about right or wrong, it is about right versus easy.

4. **Invoke Your Super Nature.**
When you do the opposite of your nature you invoke the 90% spiritual realm. Gods and goddesses do not worry about petty issues, and when you resist the urge to react according to your physical nature. Surprising changes occur and the external situations resolve themselves. Someone suddenly crashes into the individual who took your parking space. Or you get a closer parking space and parking pass. This is how supernatural powers occur when you behave as a god or goddess.

We are made in the image of the Divine but far too often we fail to exercise our divinity because we are too focused on external circumstances. In order to make miracles occur, we have to learn to resist our sahu (animal, lower self).

Understand, I am not saying ignore when someone hurts you, stabs you in the back, gets a promotion over you, cusses you out, cuts you off in traffic, take your parking space that you are waiting for, etc. This is normal to feel. It is part of the human experience. Our feelings help us to gauge and alert us to when there is a problem.

But our feelings do not determine or dictate how we should react or behave. So, acknowledge the emotions because it is part of the human experience.

Just do not react to them.

Remember, if we believe that the Divine is All Knowing and All Powerful, then the Divine is rooting for you. This means that there is really nothing to worry about. You simply have to express what you want and not worry about how it will manifest.

Know that when you act like a human being, you will receive human assistance, which we all know is not reliable. However, when you act from a divine perspective your Spirits (the Universe) will act in your favor and you receive divine assistance.

SIX:
Becoming Maa Khru (Born Again Kemetically)

In the previous chapter, we read that Oset wanted fulfillment, meaning she did not want to be told that she was great because she is made in the likeness of the Perfect Creator. She wanted to prove it to herself. She wanted to know without a shadow of doubt that she is a divine for being. She wanted to create and be the source of her own happiness. So, Oset tricked Ra who in turn created opposition for her in order to fulfill her of achieving fulfillment.

Now, the reason Oset tricked Ra into revealing his name is because the Ra moment on the maa aankh corresponds to our puberty and young adult years.

Think about it. Do you remember your childhood? Do you remember how easily you were entertained? Do you remember how the simplest things such as blowing the ripe fruit of a dandelion (the dandelion puff) just overwhelmed you with joy? Do you remember how you were surrounded with love from your parents, grandparents and others who cared about your wellbeing? For the most part, our childhood was full of joy because we did not have a care in the world.

When you look at the maa aankh, the reason children are so innocent, pure, easily entertained, naive, etc. is because they are at the Khepera moment, which is close to the Source, the original Ra, the Hidden Ra, Amun Ra.

But then something happens.

As soon as children reach puberty and become young adults, which is the Ra moment (the Visible Ra). They begin to make unwise choices and decisions based upon 1) what they learned in their previous years (the Khepera to Ra moment) and 2) what they like or dislike. In other words, they begin to live their life based totally upon their sahu (the subconscious ego-self), instinctively like animals.

Think about it.

When did you start cursing and swearing? When did you start arguing? When did you start storming off and slamming doors? When did you start hanging around the wrong crowd? When did you start having sex? When did you start smoking, drinking alcohol and experimenting with recreational drugs?

Can you see what happened? Do you see when our life started to spiral out-of-control and why most (if not all) of our problems can be traced back to the Ra moment? Now, do you understand why Oset tricked Ra into revealing his secret name?

By tricking the visible Ra into revealing his secret/hidden name or Amun Ra, she (and all of her descendants) became accountable for what occurs in our life once we reach puberty. This is the reason the Ra moment which is symbolized as the color red, corresponds to the peak of male aggressiveness and the female menstrual cycle. It should not make sense why in traditional societies, teenagers undergo rites-of-passage (initiations) in order to become responsible adults.

Most (if not all) of our problems can be traced back to this particular period in our life—the Ra moment—because this is where we become accountable for our life. It is at the Ra moment of our life, we enter into the Age of Accountability, meaning we can no longer blame Mommy and Daddy for anything going on in our life. Please understand, this does not excuse people who have harmed us during our childhood. Note that our parents, guardians, aunts, uncles, grandparents, etc. are not perfect, and have probably made some serious mistakes. So, the Ra moment does not excuse anyone who has wrong us but life does not stop either.

When Children of Oset enter into the Ra moment, regardless of what went wrong and who's to blame. We all, now have the responsibility to fix whatever is wrong.

Another interesting thing about the Ra moment is that when we get this point in our life. We also discover our metaphorical thermostat.

The Thermostat

A thermostat, as many of you know, basically controls the internal temperature of a room, house, building, etc. We like a room, house, building, etc. have an internal thermostat that regulates our body's internal temperature. However, we also have a thermostat gives us the internal capacity we need to govern every aspect of our life. For instance, the difference between a self-made wealthy person and a rich person, is that the self-made wealthy individual's wealth thermostat gives them to internal capacity to lose all of their money but make more of it. Most rich people when they lose their money, are flat broke and never recover financially because their wealth thermostat does not allow them to do so.

A self-made wealthy person who is used to making $10,000 a week because of their wealth thermostat would never be content with making $2000 a month. On the flipside, a rich person who is used to making $2000 a month, will never be content with receiving $10, 000 a week, but their wealth thermostat is not adjusted for them to handle that amount. This is the reason; most rich people spend their money on frivolous items and are in the poor house shortly after.

The same occurs in regard to our health thermostat. Have you ever talked to people that are obese about improving their health? For instance, my family, like many working-class families across the country, has a carbohydrate rich diet. As a result, many of my family members are obese. When you start talking to them about health, they all seem to say the same thing, "I know I need to eat more vegetables" but they never change their diet unless they have a health scare. The reason is because their health thermostat convinces them that they are comfortable being overweight.

We all have a thermostat regarding every aspect of our life. For most of us, our thermostat does not give us any problems. If we are comfortable, then our thermostat is at a comfortable setting. Problems arise when we want to change our thermostat. For instance, you are tired of walking up a flight of stairs huffing and puffing, so you decide to lose weight. That is when you come face to face with your thermostat and find it hard to change. Or, you are trying to get ahead financially by purchasing rental property but as the deal finalize you chicken out, and so on.

Anytime you try to do something such as accomplish a new goal, increase or improve your wellbeing and there is something you do that sabotages it. It is a sign that your thermostat needs to be adjusted.

How did we get our present thermostat?

Well, our mind is composed of several layers, which can be divided into three parts called the Ab (conscious mind), sahu (subconscious) and BA (superconscious).

The Ab (conscious mind/soul) is the part of our mind that we use to make choices and decision. The Ab also gives us the ability to muster strength, courage, self-discipline, and humility. Part of the Ab's uniqueness is that it has an uncanny ability to intuit spiritual matters. It is this unique ability that allows human beings to perceive life after death and imagine a future, which separates us from animals.

The BA is the Superconscious part of our being. You see, the BA is  the infinite, omnipotent and omniscient spark of God that exists in all living beings. The Superconscious is called numerous names like the Over Soul, the Infinite Intelligence, and the collective consciousness, the Divine Mind, the Universe, the Universal Mind and even God because it is the source of infinite wisdom, pure creativity and power. In other words, everything you want to know provided you know how to access it and retrieve it is stored in the Superconscious. The purpose of the Superconscious mind is to improve the quality of life. The BA is the divine spark that provides us with creativity, knowledge and wisdom.

The sahu is the part of our mind that governs all of our autonomous bodily functions and stores all of our memories. Because our Ab is undeveloped as a child, it is our sahu that establishes our thermostat by indiscriminately mimicking our parents, aunts, uncles, grandparents, family and friends. It was how we were raised, what school we attended, and the churches we attended. It could be the trauma, our pride, etc. that influenced our thermostat. In the end, it could be every pattern that we fall back into when something occurs. This is why the Kemetic sages called this part of our mind a jackass because while it does a lot of work. Its inability to make unwise decisions can cause it to be a hazard to our wellbeing.

Understand, if you are trying to make some improvements and you receive pushback, it is due to your sahu. The entity that dwells within your sahu (subconscious) is called Set. Set (Set-an or Satan) is the spirit of chaos, confusion and calamity. Set is not the epitome of evil but simply a malevolent and uncontrollable force that resides within us and attracts other negative forces. Simply put, Set is the entity that encourages us to do what is Easy.

Set

So, when we get to the Ra moment, we become accountable for everything that goes on in our life. When we begin to implement change, that is when we encounter the entity Set who discourages us from doing what is Right and encourages us to do what is Easy. When we follow our Set, and do what is Easy, we attract malevolent spirits that feed off of the fears, selfishness and inhibitions of our sahu, which results in us having a horrible life.

However, when we do what is Right, we awaken the entity who dwells within our BA (Superconscious) known as Osar. Osar technically speaking is our Higher Self or primary guardian angel, which is called a netcharu. More will be said about this in the near future but, when we resist the urge to be cruel, selfish, egotistical, hurting another, etc. Although doing what is Right is not Easy all the time, it readjusts us thermostat because by resisting the urge to be selfish by sharing; instead of being mean and spiteful, choosing to be kind and respectful. Our actions and behaviors attract positive forces to us that guide us to individuals who will help us in doing the Right thing.

Osar

It is very important that you understand that this is not about being nice but about doing what is Right to get Power.

Many of us (at one point in our life) ran with some negative people. We saw these people make really bad decisions that resulted in people around them getting hurt, but they were fun to be with. A lot of times, even if we knew better, we continued to hang out with them despite being told not to do so, and why? Because we did not want to hurt their feelings. We were being nice. Does it make sense now why some women knowing a guy is a thug or some men knowing a woman is a gold-digger, will compromise their principles and dignity? So understand, this is not about being nice. It is about Power.

It should be noted that doing what is Easy usually, results in further difficulties, drama and tragedies in the long run. Doing what is Right, sometimes is very hard but in the end, it is worth it.

For example, would you prefer to win a million dollar with the understanding that you would most likely waste it very shortly? Or, would you prefer to work hard to earn a million dollars knowing that it would grow exponentially in the following years and you will be able to pass that wealth to your descendants? Most people as, unappealing as it sounds, would choose the second option and this is the reason for doing what is Right, which the hero Hru discovered in the *Story of Osar*.

The Ancient African Path to Fulfillment

Since Oset wanted fulfillment, she wanted to be in control, etc. In order to grant her wish, since humankind was constantly plotting against Ra. Ra relinquished his throne according to legend to Geb (the Spirit of the Earth). This is an allusion referring to the fact that early human beings lived our lives based upon our natural instincts (see the Basic Needs of *Maslow's Hierarchy of Needs*).

But early humans found Geb to be an unfit ruler, which is an allusion referring to humanity's Physiological Needs. In other words, early human beings wanted a sense of belonging. They wanted honor, power and wealth. So it is imagined that during the Rule of Geb they wanted to organize into tribes and clans.

Eventually, Geb resigned and to satisfy Oset's desire for fulfillment because by this time, we she (we) forgot what our true godlike nature was. As instructed by Ra, Geb divided up his kingdom and relinquished it to Osar and his youngest brother Set. This is an allusion referring to the intensity and level of power; Osar is older, hence more powerful so he corresponds to the BA (Superconscious), while Set is the youngest therefore less powerful and corresponds to sahu during the Khepera and Ra moments.

Initially life as you can imagine was horrible for early human beings because in order to honor Oset's request. Life had to be made extremely difficult and filled with chaos, confusion, difficulties, disorder, illness, obstacles, setbacks and suffering. In order for us to learn how to appreciate, create, overcome, share and resolve our issues by connecting to Amun Ra, so that we can achieve fulfillment. The first individual to accomplish this feat, according to legend was Osar.

Now when Osar became king it was a horrible time because his people were at constant war with one another. Osar wanting to bring peace to his people, sought out ways to bring them together. It is said that he spoke with Ra, and upon doing so he returned to his people with a body of laws that they could use to govern themselves with.

After introducing the laws to his people, Osar learned from his wife (sister) how to cultivate plants, which laid the foundation for the science of agriculture. As the laws that Osar introduced and the science of agriculture spread throughout the land, the country quickly grew and became very prosperous and peaceful. Everyone cherished Osar and loved their king, except for his youngest brother Set who was jealous of Osar's glory, power and fame.

Seeing that everything was prospering, Osar had decided to spread his teachings throughout the world in order to help others. As he traveled the world, Oset perfectly ruled the kingdom in his absence, but unbeknownst to them both. Their younger brother Set was plotting along with 72 conspirators to assassinate Osar upon his return.

When Osar returned back home, Set held a celebration in Osar's honor, which was attended by everyone except for Oset. Along with Osar, the dignitaries and other officials dined on the food and ale that Set provided. Then when everyone was full and merry, Set had his disguised conspirators bring out a beautifully decorated chest. As everyone expressed their amazement and wonder of the beautifully decorated chest, Set promised that whoever would fit inside the chest perfectly he would award the chest to them. So, one by one each of the guests tried to lay inside the chest but the chest was either too big or not small enough. Finally when it came to Osar, the beloved king full of ale and after much persuasion decided lay inside the chest. Set knowing all along that Osar would fit perfectly inside signaled his conspirators to seal the chest and throw it in the Nile River, where the chest of Osar sank, thus killing Osar through suffocation.

As the chest sank into the Nile, no one challenged Set as he usurped the throne. Not even his older brother Hru Ur. It is said that even Ra turned his head aside and wept of the news of Osar's death, but he would not even go against his grandchild. Then Set knowing that Oset was the only one who would challenge his authority declared her a fugitive in her own kingdom.

When Oset heard what happened to Osar, she went into mourning and immediately began looking for the chest along the Nile, in order to give her husband a proper burial. Ra it is said looking from above pitied her and sent Npu (Anpu, Anubis in Greek) to help find the body of Osar's. Shortly after Npu led Oset to a group of children who told her that they saw the chest floating towards the sea. With Npu's help, Oset found that the chest had floated to Byblos. Where the chest laid, a massive tree had grown and engulfed it. The king of Byblos after hearing of this magical tree had it cut down and formed into a pillar, totally unaware of the contents within.

When Oset arrived in Byblos, after pleading with the king to cut open the pillar, so that she could recover her king, the king finally conceded. When Osar's body fell out of the chest, Oset took the body and sailed back home. It is said during this time, she was so grief stricken that in one version of the Story she changed herself into a swallow through magical means, and while swarming around the chest in morning caused Osar's member to rise through the fluttering of her wings, thus conceiving an heir. In another version, it is said that Oset lay with Osar and through magical means became pregnant. In any case, both are important to note because it is the first mention of an immaculate conception.

When Oset got back in Kemet, she secretly hid Osar's body in the marsh while she stole away to get birth to Osar's heir but, during a hunting expedition, Set stumbled upon the chest. When he opened it and saw his dead brother, in a fit of rage hacked up the corpse and spread each part all over the kingdom, except for the phallus, which was thrown in the river and eaten by a fish.

Totally unaware of Set's actions, Oset gave birth to a premature son whom she named Hru. When she finally returned to the marsh and found what Set had done. She began searching for Osar's body again, but this time after hearing about Set's rage. Nebhet accompanied Oset, Npu and Hru in their quest.

Together they searched the entire kingdom and every time they found a fragment of Osar's body. They collected and, in its place, they built a shrine to remind people that Osar's body was found here. Through these efforts because of the kingdom was so poorly managed, a great revival of Osar's kingdom had begun and began to spread. When all of the pieces were assembled, Oset through magical means created a phallus since the original member was eaten by fish.

Still longing for her husband and saddened by his lost. She mourned over the lifeless body and asked Djahuti if there was any way that he could be revived. Djahuti knowing full well that Osar's spirit had departed from his body for a while now would not recognize his deformed body. Instead Djahuti instructed Oset to wrap the body in linen so that they could give him a proper burial and that way his restless spirit could finally find peace, thus becoming the first of honorable ancestors.

There were many attempts made on Hru when he was a child, but when he had come of age. Osar appeared to him in a dream and inspired the young prince to avenge his wrongful death.

Hru gathered supporters for his army and inspired by the dream challenged Set in battle. Set being the older and more experienced in war would lose a few battles but managed to defeat Hru on the battlefield. Then in a desperate attempt to kill Set, Hru managed to get close to his adversary but was quickly defeated and in the process Set gouged Hru's eye[5] out.

Unable to see, Hru and his forces were forced to retreat and he fled to see Djahuti, the only one whom Set feared.

---

[5] Remember the Aakhut or right Utchat (Eye of Ra) represents information controlled by the left hemisphere of the brain. Set gouging Hru's eye is an allusion referring to the fact that all information does not come from external sources.
[6] The Aabit or left Utchat (Eye of Ra) represents information processed by the right hemisphere of the brain. Osar's appearance is an allusion regarding spiritual insight.

Djahuti repaired Hru's eye perfectly[6] which is an allusion that Hru now had insight, wisdom, etc. When Hru met Set on the battlefield this time. The young courageous prince managed to cut the seat of Set's pants and subdued Set's forces. After defeating Set, Hru dragged Set to be judged to the true ruler of the land that he recognized, his mother Oset. But Oset refused to cast judgment on Set on the grounds that Set was family. Disgusted by her decision he set Set free and cut Oset's diadem.

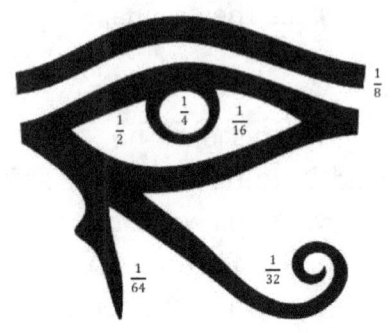

Although Set was defeated on the battlefield he still held sway over the land, so he launched a campaign against Hru attesting to his legitimacy. Set traveled throughout the kingdom claiming that Hru was not Osar's heir, which eventually caused the conflict between the two to be brought before a tribunal.

When the tribunal convened to deliver justice, they could not decide who to rule in favor of. Just like the war, the complaint between Set about Hru would not be resolved in a simple and quick judgment. The case between the two lasted for what seemed like forever as the supporters of each on the tribunal bickered among themselves.

To bring the entire matter to a close, Djahuti made the suggestion (according to one version) that Osar speak on Hru's behalf. When Osar appeared[7], he spoke as Tum (an enlightened spirit) from beyond the grave stating how disappointed he was in their inability to make a fair, just and quick decision. He reminded the tribunal how he grew to prominence by introducing laws, burial rites and the science of agriculture to his people. He reminded them that before he had done any of this that his people.

They were all living in wickedness, which was the state that the kingdom had degraded back into under Set's rule. Osar told the tribunal that he was not a hypocrite that told people to do something but didn't follow the rules himself. He reminded them that he was just and that it was because of his righteous living he became the Lord of the Underworld. Osar explained that this was due to Set destroying the Halls of Maa he had built, which resulted in the great hall being rebuilt in the Underworld.
In closing Osar told the tribunal that if they did not make a just decision shortly, they would all see justice in the Underworld when they die.

The tribunal met after Osar's spiel and didn't hesitate to rule in Hru's favor, while Set was found to be guilty. Hru was declared because he was found to be maa khru (true of voice) and recognized as the true heir of the Osar. Consequently, Hru was awarded the double Pschent crown while Set was punished to travel around the world, telling people about his misdeeds and how Osar and Hru united the kingdom.

The Truth about the Story of Osar

As you have probably already figured it out, ever since Set usurped the throne of Osar, there has been disease, illness, plague, pestilence, jealousy, war, loss of love, tragedy and misery because Set corresponds to the Ra moment. He is described as the youngest sibling to indicate that he is at the Ra moment (the Age of Accountability), where instead of doing what is Right, he does what is Easy. The Ra moment, you will recall is the peak of male aggressiveness (also the moment when young women begin their menses), it is where most of our problems in life begins. Set is the primary foe spirit of Chaos, Confusion, Calamity, Uncertainty, etc., hence the ruler of TASETT, and he is perched on your left shoulder (corresponding to the left-hemisphere of the brain).

Osar brings love, unity, family, children, knowledge, wisdom, wealth, prosperity and long life because he corresponds to the Amun Ra moment on the maa aankh. He is the eldest sibling to indicate that once he got to the Ra moment (the Age of

Accountability). He chose to do what is Right instead of what is Easy. The Amun Ra moment, you will recall is the peak of spiritual prowess. It is where we find clarity, knowledge, wisdom and understanding of why we are here and our purpose. Osar is our primary guardian spirit of Peace, Prosperity, Knowledge, Wellbeing, Certainty etc., hence the Lord of the Underworld or KAMTA, and he rests on your right shoulder (corresponding to the right-hemisphere of the brain).

Hru symbolizes us, the Children of Oset, who are responsible for their lives and have the power to make decisions and choices, by uniting both brothers. In other words, by following our Osar, we are able to naturally align our Set.

It is important to understand that Set is not the epitome of evil or the chief adversary who rebels against his Creator as in Christian myth. He exists to help us to understand our strengths and weaknesses. Remember, we derive fulfilment only from what we earn, so Set exist to oppose us, for our own betterment.

Set places a sense of urgency on our development because we have all been given a specific time to accomplish our destiny (purpose) in this life time. If we do not achieve our ultimate goal, then we must return and do it in another life time.

Therefore, when we do what is Easy (e.g. cheating, stealing, gossiping, lying, etc.) instead of what is Right, three things happen:

1. We attract more Setian (negative forces) to us and repel the Osarian (benevolent forces) surrounding us.
2. Since we did not develop the skills required to obtain and maintaining the thing we want. The thing that came to us

easy never lasts long and gives us a temporary moment of joy and many times a long-term headache.
3. Most importantly, we miss the opportunity to achieve fulfillment or the sense of accomplishment, which is the reason why we are here.

Lesson Six: Recognizing Your Set

Most people have a twisted idea about destiny because it has been influenced by fiction writers and mythological movies. In these movies, we always see or hear of some wise guru telling a young hero or heroine that they are destined to saving the world and ridding the planet of all sorts of problems. Unfortunately, the

wise guru never tells the protagonists of the story what they have to overcome in order to achieve their destiny. The reason for this is because if the sagely teacher mentioned any of this, the young hero would give up. This is the reason no one can accurately define what your purpose is in because it is all dependent on you.

This is why in the Kemetic *Story of Osar*, the ultimate goal is described as the prize or Hru's birthright. If you really want to know what you came here to accomplish, simply choose something you want to

That being said, the opposition you face in regard to achieving any goal will cause your Set to appear. Set will always present you with what is Easy versus what is Right. Set is the spirit of chaos, confusion and storms so, if you look at your life. You can identify his presence by finding the areas in your life that have no order. Also, most events where you find yourself being anxious, worrisome or fearful, especially of events that occurred in the past, are also signs that Set has blinded you in that area of your life.

In this exercise, list all of the issues you struggle with. Include scenarios and situations that you find yourself in, where you tell yourself that you cannot do something. For instance, Set will always give you an excuse to convince you that you cannot achieve a goal that others have accomplish.

Ritual to Overcome Set

In the *Story of Osar*, Hru became Maa Khru (Born Again) after he relinquished control to Osar, thus allowing him to intercede on his behalf. Maa Khru means to be Free!

This is not easy for many of us to do because many of us have been conditioned to believe that we are powerless, like the elephant who has been conditioned to believe that he cannot break rope that binds him. But, many of us are beginning to discover that most of what we have learned about the Divine and our self, is an extremely interpretation of our ancient ancestors' spirituality. In order to reclaim our birthright, we have to remove the chains of mental and spiritual bondage.

Now if you are thinking that it was dummied down to make Black people more subservient. That is incorrect. No. It was dummied down thousands of years ago, by the attendees of the Council of Nicaea in 325 A.D. Here, emperor Constantine along with a council of Christian bishops argued, debated and voted to make Jesus of Nazarene, the literal and only "Son of God."

And, ever since that great historic day, instead of people seeing the Father as their Superconscious (or Higher Self), Jesus as their Conscious (or Soul) and the Holy Ghost as the whole mind

(Superconscious-Conscious-Subconscious), as the early Christian writers. Christianity under the leadership of Constantine, the Vatican and later other heads (and religious heads) of state, became a tool for social control. That dictates to mindless religious zealots and robots how to do everything including, eat, breathe and live. Does it now make sense why the most religious people in the world have been found to be the most hypocritical, scandalous, sexually perverted, tyrannical and corrupt people in the world?

When you truly understand why these bishops were so hell-bent on deifying Jesus. It becomes crystal clear why Christianity cosigned the annihilation of indigenous Americans, the enslavement of Africans and desecration of the African continent and the slaughter of women and children who were accused of witchcraft, and numerous other atrocities.

Unfortunately, because Western societies are built upon the Judeo-Christian belief system. Learning about the true history of Christianity or reading about the heinous crimes committed to this day by members in the clergy, is still not enough to break the chains of indoctrination. This is because Judeo-Christian beliefs permeate every aspect of Western culture and are perpetuated in books, music and film. For instance, I know people who have not been to church in ages and have adopted new belief systems. But, the idea of heaven and hell still frightens them and they still believe in the apocalypse.

Therefore, the purpose of initiation is to shake chains of indoctrination off so that as this Setian world we live in comes to an end. You have full confidence and a stable, peace of mind knowing that you will not cease to exist with it.

For many, some extraordinary and remarkable event must by physically observed in order to convince us that we are responsible for our salvation. This remarkable event also must convince us that we are not alone and that we need to dedicate our life to becoming one with the Divine in order to improve our life.

Historically speaking, this remarkable event may have been a deathly illness, near death experience, a powerful and profound visit from a dead relative in your dreams or some other profound experience. If you are reading this book, most likely you have already had this experience. However, to mark your initiation, you need something so bizarre, so mysterious (if not horrifying), to reboot your sahu (subconscious), in order for you to see your Osar and other spirits. You cannot just light some candles and suddenly declare yourself reborn. I wish it were that easy but then again, if it were it would not be worth it. You have to have an inciting incident. Because I am fond of rituals, I have experimented with several. The most powerful one I have found and used is a modification of an initiation rite written in Paul Huson's *Mastering Witchcraft,* which involves reciting the *Lord's Prayer* backwards.

Huson insisted that the original rite be conducted for three consecutive nights for "initiation" only, by candlelight before going to bed, while visualizing chains around the ankles and wrists being struck by lightning as the prayer is read backwards. Thus, turning the chains into molten shards as they fall to the ground.

My modification of the ritual consist of taking a machete, sword, or knife (if neither can be found, one can visualize it). Then, decorate the tool in the colors of the guardian spirit of protection and revolution, Hru Aakhuti (blood red or blood red and purple). Then, instead of visualizing lightening break the chains, use the weapon to hack and cut the invisible chains of bondage from between one's legs, around the wrists and head. As you hack at the bondage, see Hru Aakhuti's glowing fire break the chains.

1. Draw the maa aankh as instructed in Chapter 2.
2. Light a red candle.
3. Call upon Hru Aakhuti and his warrior spirits to remove the chains of bondage from your being.
4. Make an offering of rum, cigar smoke or whatever you feel your Hru Aakhuti would accept.
5. Spray the machete with rum.
6. Blow smoke on the machete.
7. Read the Lord's Prayer phonetically as follows:

NEMA! LIVEE, MORF SU REVILLED TUB NOISHAYTPMET OOTNI TON SUH DEEL SUS TSHAIGA SAPSERT TAHT YETH. VIGRAWF EU ZA SESAPSERT RUA SUH VIGRAWF DERB ILAID RUA YED SITH SUH VIG NEVEH NI SI ZA THRE NI NUD EEB LIW EYTH MUCK MODNGIK EYTH MAIN EYTH EEB DWOHLAH NEVAH NI TRA CHIOO. RETHARF RUA!

8. Sits quietly and contemplate what comes to your awareness. If anything, angry, destructive or indignant comes to mind. Write it down and invoke Hru Aakhuti to destroy it by placing it on the weapon and burning it in the candle flame.
9. Thank Hru Aakhuti for his assistance and close the ritual.

I have found this rite to be helpful in removing any restricting and limited belief, as well as fears associated with dogmatic religions. It may be helpful after performing this rite that as soon as these indoctrinating and limiting beliefs appear that you write them down, such as, turn the other cheek, the so-called Golden Rule or "do unto others as you want them to do unto you", etc. It is important that you understand that these beliefs, which are controlling how you act, behave and live, are also restricting you from achieving your potential, limiting you from enjoying your life and allowing you to be preyed upon by others who do not share the same beliefs.

Let me say again, that the purpose of this rite is not to conjure up Satan but to undo the crippling damage caused by the Judeo-Christian belief system that has been imposed upon many of us since birth. That being said, use common sense. Do not burn the candle near flammable objects and do not use the weapon to hurt yourself or others. I, nor the publisher are not responsible for your actions or behaviors.

Successful performance of this ritual will result in many of the negative personality traits such as, fear, guilt, shame, etc. to come to one's awareness, so that they can be flung away from one's being. Successful completion of this rite would allow you to be closer to what Nebertcher intended you to be, which is free.

Successful completion of this rite may also require you to observe certain taboos. Note that many of these taboos will prevent you from reverting back to your old ways.

SEVEN:
Creating a Magickal Way of Life

My brother told me a story of this man who was taught that prayer changes everything, so when his rent was due on the coming Tuesday. On Friday, he prayed and prayed for God to give him the money he needed to pay his rent. He prayed all day Saturday, Sunday and Monday and come Tuesday, as he was waiting for his miracle. His landlord walked into the house and took his belongings and placed them neatly on the curve.

We have all heard stories similar to this where people pray for a miracle and the request is not answered at all. Or, the request is answered with dubious requirements, like the woman who prays for a good man, but loses him because she does not know how to keep him.

Preventive and Triage (Emergency) Magick

The above are examples of what I call triage or emergency magick. Triage or emergency magick is similar to going to the ER (emergency room) at a hospital, where the medical staff sees broken limbs or a gushing blood. The immediate response is to react and mend the limb or stop the bleeding. In other words, it is like patching you up, which is the reason the medical professional says once you leave the ER, "Make sure you see your primary physician." In other words, emergency or triage magick is usually sloppy magick.

This is how most people do their magickal and spiritual work. They wait until the last minute and that is when they want to pull out the stops and perform magickal acts or ask for divine assistance. In other words, most people function from the premise that "if it ain't broke don't fix it." This is not good magickal or spiritual practice because usually when an emergency occurs, most people are in a panic. As a result, the magickal or spiritual practices are sloppy, poorly planned and poorly executed.

For instance, if you talk to anyone who does magickal or spiritual work, they all have a story of how they used their divine skills to get them out of a financial pinch. But, I have yet to hear these people mention how they used their divine skills to prevent financial emergencies from occurring. In other words, how many times have you heard of people doing an abundance ritual when they get paid or get a large sum of money? Rarely, if not at all, right?

This is not how our ancestors lived their way of life. The reason it is a cultural saying to "put God first" is because our aakhu understood that God was not the Supreme Being but our Osar, who is associated with our BA (Superconscious). They ritualized every aspect of their life in order to ensure that their BA was fully engaged. This is the reason there was a ritual for practically everything.

Unfortunately, because the philosophy was lost, many of us have gotten out of the habit of putting our God, our Spirits, Osar, Ancestors, etc. first because of the distaste we have for Christianity. Some of us due to a lack of metaphysical training refuse to put "God first" because it is seen as a mystery God concept. While others have chosen not to do this because of our misunderstanding about the nature of importance of both the material and spiritual world.

But, being spiritual practitioners we need to get back in the habit of first, calling upon the spiritual forces that surround us then proceeding with the physical work to accomplish the project. So the purpose of this chapter is to present a few practices that can be performed weekly, monthly and annually, along with miscellaneous rituals.

The Ultimate Test of Faith

If you are working with spirits but you were not born into this spiritual culture, you will eventually come to a point where you will ask yourself regardless of what you have learned "Are spirits real?"

This question will make you question if your spiritual work is worth it or if it is just a waste of time. You may even go through a period of reading and rereading books about spirituality, spirits, ancestors, etc. to assure yourself that what you are doing is beneficial to your wellbeing. In this situation, you are being put to the test and pressured to prove that your spirits are real and that it is not all in your head. This will be compounded by the fact that you will meet or interact with people who will try to discourage you in any way they can.

This is a crossroad situation in which your spirits are testing you to see if you are for real about spiritual development or if it is just a passing fad. This situation occurs to everyone and is heightened if you live with someone who is not into this type of spirituality such as a spouse or relative that is very religious, and if there is a lack of money. Rest assure, this happens to everyone and here are some appropriate responses when it occurs:

1. **"Your Spirits are not real."** First, you do not need to prove anything to anyone except for yourself. Can Christians,

Muslims and Jews prove that God or Allah exists? No, so why should you have to prove that your Spirits do? You don't. So, do not get goaded into silly debates regarding what is real and what is not. Know that your Spirits are real to you and that is all that matters.

2. **"Why Do You Have an Altar?"** This is a common question you will get especially from nosy religious family members who feel they have the right to ask you anything. The nice and short response is "Because it allows me to focus and talk to God." This usually shuts them down because it is specific and vague enough to make them ponder. If they persist, then simply say, "The same reason why there are altars inside your church."

3. **"Why do you worship the ancestors?"** The ancestors are not worship but honored. Aside from venerating and remembering those who made sacrifices for us to be here. The reason for honoring the ancestors is for spirit communication. Our ancestors and spirit guides or aakhu are our personal angels and the first line of defense against negative influences. There are numerous reports that have been collected from around the world of deceased relatives giving warnings, guidance and sagely advice to their living loved ones. Therefore, the reason we honor our aakhu is to maintain this positive relationship, so that they will continue to assist us in our life.

4. **"Why do you worship gods and goddesses?"** The netcharu are not gods and goddesses but guardian spirits like guardian angels, which is the reason they are not worship. Only the Divine, our Perfect Creator is worshipped. The purpose of honoring the netcharu is to remind ourselves

that we can call upon them at any time because they have been assigned to govern a particular area of our life.

5. **"How come you cannot just call upon Jesus?"** The reason we do not call upon Jesus is because according Judeo-Christian belief, Jesus is called upon to save humankind from sin, not to help with employment, help with a test, improve relationships between spouses, increase one's luck, improve finances, etc. In other words, Jesus deals specifically with salvation and not with our daily affairs. The Spirits help us with our everyday affairs.

6. **"Why do you burn candles and make offerings to the Spirits?"** We live in a world of constant change where nothing received freely is appreciated. To show that we appreciate a blessing received, we make offerings in return for our blessings so that we do not misuse what was given.

7. **"Isn't what you are doing evil?"** If we accept that God is the Creator of All Things, then God does not see it as evil because it would contradict the nature of God. It is mankind who separates people and things and has classified what is good and evil, not God.

8. **Why do you do magick?** The reason we do magick is because telling your sahu (lower self) to do something is ineffective a lot of times. For instance, if you were a smoker and told yourself that you were going to stop smoking. Or, if you overeat and you tell yourself you are going to stop eating so much. You would find that after telling yourself those commands, they do not work because these destructive behaviors are deeply ingrained into your lower spirit (sahu). So magick is employed to

move our lower spirit and it is also used to get tangible physical results as well.

9. **Why do you do rituals?** Sobonfu Some' says it best, "Ritual keeps us connected to our spirit, our soul and our purpose."

10. **Why don't you just put it all in God's hands?** We believe that we were created in the image of the Divine so that we can experience an earthly life and develop our divine powers. Therefore, every problem, every obstacle, every setback, etc. is like lifting weights for your spirits because it gives an opportunity to spiritually grow by tapping into the BA – the Divine Spark – within us and communing with our Spirits to resolve our problems. Spiritual muscles or power does not come from relinquishing total control to the Divine, it comes from fulfillment, which means we must earn it.

    Just like in life, if our parents stepped in and bailed us out of every bind, we got in. We would become entitled brats, who would not learn how to appreciate hard work but also not develop into mature, responsible and accountable adults. In the same sense, if the Divine stepped in and saved us would not develop into mature, responsible and accountable divine beings or gods and goddesses (angels, ancestors, etc.).

    Some things we do put in the Divine's or our Spirits' hands, but for the most part, we believe that we are responsible for our own salvation.

How to Build Up Your Spiritual Bank

A spiritual bank is basically a reserve of blessings that you acquire from doing what is Right versus what is Easy. We all have a spiritual bank that we acquire in this lifetime. Basically, the way a spiritual bank works is that more you do what's right, the most spiritual blessings you acquire. Whenever you get something freely, it is because of your spiritual bank. It is sort of like your Spirits see you from the other side struggling and decide to help you out. For those who have watched the film the *Hunger Games*, these spiritual blessings are like the silk parachuted donations the tributes received from sponsors. The Sponsors could be seen as our Spirits.

This is because your actions and behaviors increase your Rau or more specifically your personal ra.

Have you ever noticed that some people seem to be luckier than others? Have you ever noticed that for some people, things seem to work out for them all the time? For instance, I began this book talking about my wife and my desire to have a child. Just to give a little insight, we do not have any family that lives near us. We also do not have a lot of friends, but out of the blue. When people heard that we were expecting a baby, our coworkers decided to throw us a baby shower. We were a little worried about purchasing items but gifts came in from all over the country supporting our child. And, when I say gifts, I am not just talking about little gifts like baby rattles. We received all sorts of gifts and quite a few of them were very expensive. It was because my wife and I have both made contributions (in time, money, energy, etc.) without asking for nothing in return.

Most people misunderstand the law of reciprocity because they have been taught that it is all about being nice or "treating others as you want to be treated", hence commonsense or the golden rule, but this is not correct.

Remember, it was because of Oset per Kemetic legend, who opened the way for humanity to transcend his or her animalistic nature and tap into the BA – the Divine Spark. In other words, Oset opened the way for us to become gods and goddesses. She put our salvation in our hands, so we do not have to wait for God to save us. By having the hidden name of Ra revealed, she put us in direct contact with the Source of Creation, Amun Ra.

Amun Ra (depending on how you look at the maa aankh) is above TASETT, which means that from the Amun Ra moment perspective. Most matters are considered trivial to God. However, we have the power within us to solve our problems ourselves. This means that Oset created the science of agriculture because she was looking for ways to help people eat. She taught this science to Osar who in turn taught the entire country. So, the Kemetic Divine Feminine is about DIY – Doing It Yourself.

Think about that for a moment.

Most of the things that people bother the Divine with are trivial. If you have read books about ancient African spirituality, you would have come across that the reason most traditional Africans do not pray directly to the Supreme Being is because it is assumed that the Divine is busy managing universes. It is considered an insult to bother the Supreme Being and Perfect Creator with simple human problems. This is like asking the president of the country who is concerned with balancing the national deficit, improving the nation's education system, etc., being asked to help you with something real minor. Note that the fact that the current president of the United States regularly engages in trivial matters reveals a true lack of spiritual maturity. African rulers would never stoop to such a position because they are imitating the Creator.

So instead of What Would Jesus Do? We need to ask ourselves"

"What Would a God/Goddess Do?"

Therefore, when a person flips you off, your spouse is being argumentative, you got passed over again for promotion, etc. Ask yourself "What Would a God/Goddess Do?"

A God or Goddess would ignore it and are be nice because they are investing in their spiritual bank, which is where their greatest reward comes from.

Your rent is due, you have bills mounting up, no food and no money to pay. From the Ra moment perspective, you would worry how you are going to make ends meet but, from an Amun Ra moment perspective, from a God or Goddess perspective. You ignore it and know that things are going to work-out because you are investing in your spiritual bank and increasing your ra. This is how ancestors, saints, gods and goddesses come into being, they are self-made.

The more proactive we are, the more we increase our personal ra. The more reactive we are, the more we deplete our personal ra. Every time we resist the urge to react in a destructive, egotistical Setian perspective (the Ra moment), we increase our ra (personal power).

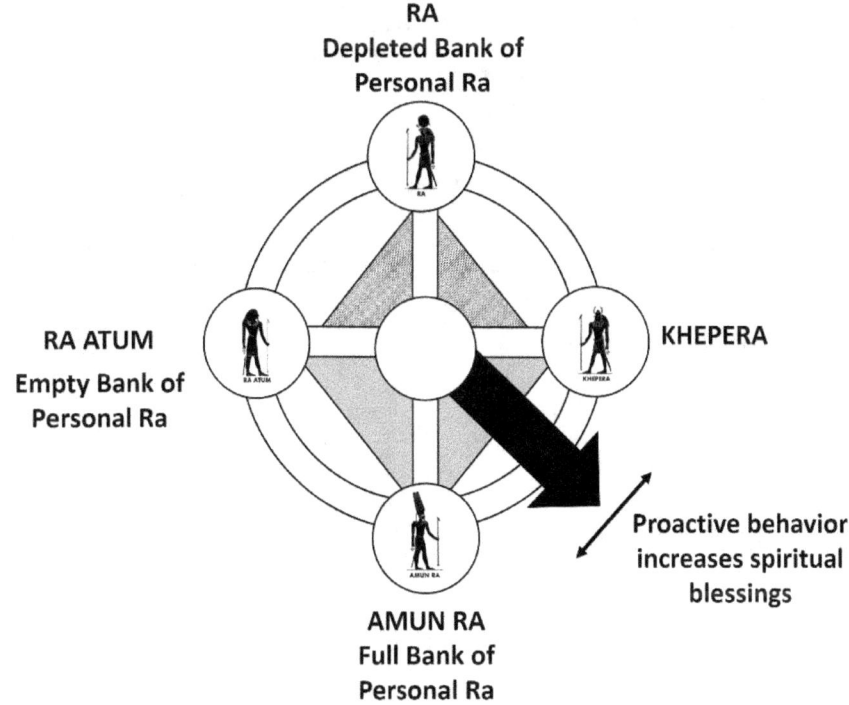

When our ra increases, we have better luck, better opportunities, better health, increased wealth, etc. because we are tapping into the Source – Amun Ra – The Hidden Ra (Source). Optimal proactive behavior is between Amun Ra and Khepera. Most people will not be perfectly proactive – Amun Ra – because we all have a physical body and must react to some things, which is the reason this position is symbolized by the Spirits.

When we are reactive, we experience greater losses, declining health, bad luck, and the lists goes on, moving towards the Ra

Atum moment, which is the marker for death. Dangerous reactive behavior is between Ra and Ra Atum.

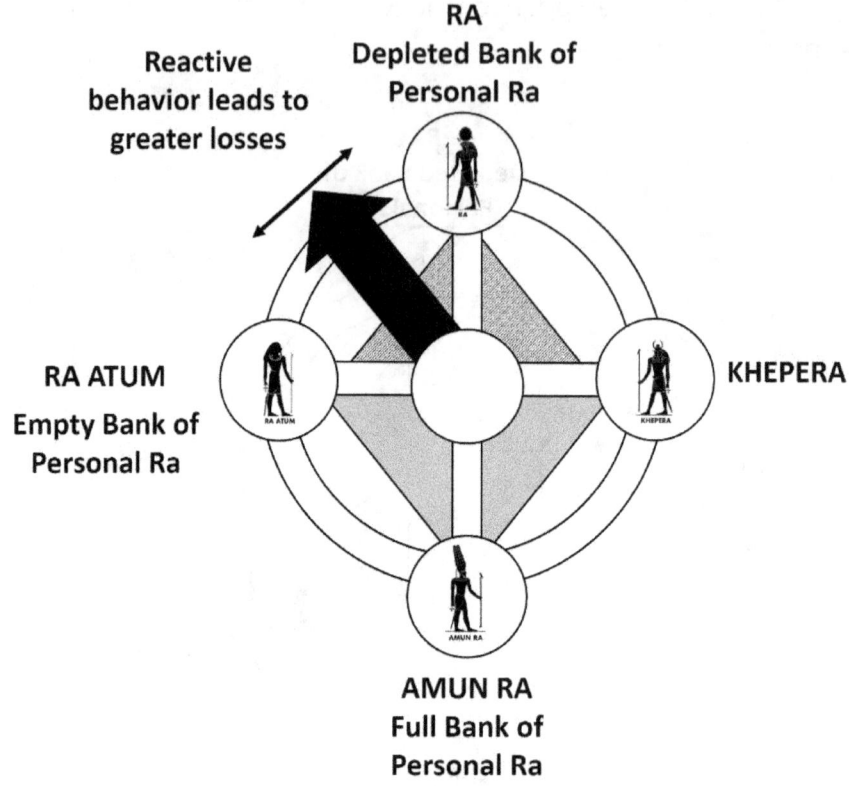

Therefore, create a proactive cultural way of life for yourself. Many indigenous and non-Western cultures incorporate this concept into their daily life by making offerings for everything. It does not matter who the offerings are made to. For instance, some cultures make the offering to their ancestors, others to the earth spirits or Mother Earth and Father Sky (or vice versa); some cultures give 10 percent of their harvest, while in the West people give ten percent of their earnings or tithes. It is all based upon the same idea of being proactive and investing in your spiritual power.

Do not err in thinking that this is just about being nice, it is about ascending to Amun Ra. Being nice adds to your ra, but being nice in the face of opposition causes your ra to grow leaps and bounds due to compound and interest.

Now that you understand this, it should be clear why charities exist. This is also the reason indigenous cultures from around the world, are in the habit of making offerings for everything because they know it adds to their spiritual bank. This is also the reason many people who understand this concept or were raised in cultures based upon this concept, do not like accept anything from free. It is not about being prideful but they know that everything has a price and things given freely, are easily lost. So, they will prefer to work, pay or offer something of equivalent value in exchange for a gift received.

Some people get hung up on who and where. For instance, they may offer some money to a beggar or some charity, who uses the funds inappropriately. This creates a bitterness about giving. Don't do it. What they do with the funds is not your concern. Of course, if you are aware that they are doing this you should avoid making offering, so as not to fund their destructiveness. But, remember you are investing in your spiritual bank. You are not doing this for notoriety.

If it upsets you and you just feel like you must know what your funds are being used for, thereby messing up your spiritual investment. There are more ways to offer charity. You can go to a grocery store and leave money in different parts of the store. For instance, place a $20 bill under an apple and stuff a $20 bill in a bunch of grapes, then leave. Don't concern yourself who gets it. Know that you are investing in your spiritual bank and your blessings come from the Source – Amun Ra.

Another thing. Don't give and say, "Well, I gave so I expect ____." The Amun Ra moment does not work on the quid pro quo system per se, which is the reason I keep calling it a spiritual investment. If you study some of the wealthiest individuals in the world, who made their wealth from stocks. They will tell you that the way to money in stocks is to continue purchasing stocks over an extended period. Smart investors will tell you that you should not look for a return in your investment for at least about ten years. That means put your money into a fund that will purchase stocks and forget about it, for at least ten years. After ten years, then look at your investment and see how much it has grown.

Well, your ra or spiritual investment works the same way. It grows and grows but when you desperately need it. You cannot be righteous, then look for the return of being righteous. That's like watching water boil. You must get in the habit of being righteous and just do it. Then, when you need a payoff, that's when the boon comes in. For instance, all the gifts my wife and I received for our baby was because we needed it. We discussed how we were going to get these things and because none of our family was around. There was no one to talk to about it or help us to purchase these things, but we had faith that things would work out. We did not worry about it. In other words, "What Would a God/Goddess Do?" A god or goddess would not worry about it. That's when our boon occurred.

Keep in mind that our Spirits are like our Sponsors, and they will parachute us what we need and, so long as we remember that we are investing in our ra.

Lesson Seven: Regular Rituals

Daily Prayer to Your BA

Remember, that your ultimate ally is your BA, so you should get into a habit of talking to your BA daily. One of the best ways to remember your BA is by expressing your gratitude for everything that you have. It does not matter what you call your BA. Since the BA is associated with Osar, I often call it Osar but if that does not meet your fancy call your BA, the Lord. In fact, if you do not know how to pray or need a formal prayer to follow. I would suggest using the Psalms. One of the best books on the subject is Robert Laremy's *The Psalm Workbook*. Simply substitute the Lord for BA or vice versa. Try it, you will be amazed how simple it and effective it is.

New Beginning Rituals

Now that you have become acclimated to the two worlds that constitute our reality. It is customary that you try to incorporate and imbue the spiritual influence into the physical world as much as possible. One of the traditional ways this is done is by offering your Spirits some of your meal every day. To perform this small rite, simply prepare your food as normal, but before consuming. Say a small prayer and inform your spirits to have some of your meal. Next wait and when you feel as if they have absorbed some of the essence. You can now consume your meal. People who practice this rite have commented that they noticed that their meal feels different as if it had been blessed.

If you choose not to share your meal with your Spirits this way, you can before you consume your meal, take a spoonful of each item from you plate and separate it from what you will consume. This can be done inconspicuously as well. Then, return to eating your meal being mindful not to eat the amount offered to your Spirits.

The whole idea of pouring liquor to Spirits stems from this same practice. Before drinking any liquor, offer your Spirits a shot by either pouring it on the ground or simply leaving a small shot glass for the Spirits. After this is done, you can resume your drinking.

These practices were initially performed as precautionary measures to prevent bad luck and harm from falling upon an individual. The practical reason behind offering food and liquor to the Spirits before consuming was to ensure that you did not overeat and was always grateful for what you had. The spiritual reason for this practice is that the Spirits could give warning about the food because sometimes that last bite or last drink could be fatal.

Many of these practices were developed during a time when poison was administered through food. By offering food to the spirit first, it is believed that they will inform you if you should not consume the food. Liquor is offered so that the drinking parties or friends are not tricked and become enemies, as what occurred with Osar and Set.

How to Open the Way with Npu (Weekly)
Assuming you honor your aakhu on a weekly basis. One of the best ways to improve your luck is by honoring Npu. This can be done for general luck and general health. Simply, light a white birthday candle and offer a shot glass of water (for the spirits of Npu). Next ask Npu to bless you with good luck and good health, by removing obstacles in your path. Then, take an egg and rub it all over your body from head to toe. Imagine the egg absorbing all of the negativity from your life. Finally, offer the egg to Npu and three puffs of cigar smoke. Note, that instead of an egg you can offer a few pieces of candy.

Finding Lost Items with Npu

Npu is the netchar you will usually work with the most because his realm of influence is everywhere. Here is a simple ritual that can be adapted with any of the netchars. To find a lost item you would go to Npu and say, "Npu I need some help in finding _____." Then, begin looking for the lost item. If the item is around, he will lead you to the place where the item has been misplaced.

Once you find the lost item. Attribute the success of you finding this item to Npu, so offer him something that he is fond of like a few pieces of candy, etc. to show your gratitude. That's it.

Again, I must restate that the spirits do not want your soul. They do not want you to offer up your child like Abraham. They do not want a contract signed in blood. This is all horror film and religious propaganda. In fact, spirits are not going to ask you to do something that will compromise your ethics or something you are uncomfortable with. They will only request that you do something per your understanding.

Weekly Resurrection Plant Ritual

Resurrection plants also known as Rose of Jericho, is a desert plant native to North Africa. The plant dries into a ball when it is dehydrated but opens when submerged in water. Spiritually the plant is used for several reasons but is best for absorbing negative influences.

To absorb negative influences, place the dried plant in a glass bowl of water (preferably clear). Issue a simple command over the plant to absorb all negative influences in your home. Then, place the bowl in the living room or near the front door. When the water in the bowl turns brown, it is working. Every Friday, you can either discard the water, pour fresh water in the bowl and repeat the command to absorb negative influences. Or, what some people do, pour fresh water in the bowl without discarding the old water, and sprinkle a few drops around the house.

Money Rituals

One thing that spiritual minded people need to get in the habit of doing money blessing rituals. Most spiritual minded people do not do money rituals because they think it is mundane but we live in a society that operates with money. Money is needed to buy food, clothes and shelter, which means we need money to physically survive. As a spiritual minded individual, it is important that we understand that money is a spirit and like most spirits. Money wants time and energy, which means that if you ignore, neglect and disrespect Money. Money will ignore, neglect and disrespect you. If, however, you appreciate, love and respect Money, Money will appreciate, love and respect you too.

To appreciate, love and respect Money, I would suggest that you honor the netchar who assist in maintaining money, namely Npu, Oset, Hru Aakhuti and Maat.

Npu is called upon to increase your luck and finances; Oset to ensure that all your needs are met; Hru Aakhuti to assist you in advancing your finances, and Maat to help you to maintain what you have, help you live in moderation and not in excess.

Afterwards, as usual give an offering for their assistance.

In addition to this, I strongly recommend that you learn how to manage your money so that you can use a proportion of it to invest in what you are interested in. There are numerous ways that this can be accomplished. For instance, you can dedicate 60% of your paycheck to paying bills and then take 10% for household items including food and gas. Then, take another 10% and use it for emergency money, 10% can go to charitable organizations of your choice (so that you are not guilted or goaded into making donations), and 10% for investments.

If this does not work for you try another. The point is that the Spirits will bail us out of financial emergencies but they expect us to learn from our lessons, so they will not keep doing it all the time. Remember, part of the reason we are here is to become responsible for our wellbeing and that includes our finances. I do not know about you but, I would rather take a proactive stance by asking my Spirits to help me turn a $100 into a $1000, then $0 to $100. Hope that makes sense.

Parting Words

The Western world seriously has it twisted, which is the reason they see mythology as entertainment. True spiritually inclined individuals understand that mythology is a blueprint of how to get the Divine to move through us. For more information on how to achieve any goal, simply study mythology and see how it relates to your situation. If you take mythology literally, you will see it as a strange and entertaining story. However, if you understand the mythology from a metaphorical perspective, you will see it as a guide to empowering your ra. This is the reason shamans do not adhere to any dogma, Dogmas place limitations on an individual's Ba-Ab-sahu, hence spirit. Shamans are openminded and respects the Spirits of every culture, so that they can help others when needed.

As we bring this to a close, I hope you realize how powerful you are and come to understand that you can change your life at will. We are all in a very powerful and life changing position where we can change the world. Gone are the days of just being good and accepting our fate. At any time, you can call upon your Spirits to assist you and others in anything because you are made in the image of the Divine. This makes you a divinity as well or a demigod and demigoddess. Yes, all the myths were written about you, so embrace it and use it to empower yourself and your loved ones.

Now, go out and change your world.

Appendix

Suggested Evocations:

Prayer for Papa and Uncle Aakhu
Remember, Papa and Uncle aakhu are the spirits of the first young African men who were enslaved and brought to North America, which meant they remember their youthful life in Africa. Whenever, I think of these spirits, the one thought that comes to mind is that they wanted to return home either physically or spiritually. They were not content and feeble as Harriet Beecher Stowe portrays them in *Uncle Tom's Cabin*. Sidebar: Josiah Henson, the man who inspired Stowe's story, escaped from slavery and fled to Canada where he established a settlement and labor school for other fugitive slaves. This is why it is important to understand that the stereotypical images most people have about African people was part of a propaganda scheme.

The real Papa and Uncles were men who wanted to be in control of their own destiny and free of the numerous abuses they suffered, which meant when they were younger. They most likely either ran away, plotted their escape or assisted others in running away to find their freedom but, for whatever reason, such as their loved ones, etc. They sacrificed their escape for freedom by remaining on the plantation, where they aged and became elderly men.

Thus, many of them have a profound knowledge of the forests and a mystical knowledge, which they brought from Africa. While on the plantation they honed their skills for a better day. For instance, if they were blacksmiths, they mastered the skill, so that one day they could use it to build the life they wanted. This is the fighting, entrepreneurial, innovative and hardworking spirit that led to the creation of numerous thriving Black townships such as Fort Mose and Rosewood in Florida, North Brentwood and Glenarden in Maryland; Freedman's Village in Virginia; Boley, Greenwood and Tulsa the infamous Black Wall Street in Oklahoma; Seneca Village and Weeksville in New York; Mound Bayou in Mississippi, Blackdom in New Mexico, and many others. Papa and Uncle aakhu need to know that the sacrifices that they made were not in vain. If they feel that they remained on the plantation for you to live your life frivolously without any regards for family and/or culture. They can become very bitter and refuse to assist you in the basic of ancestral needs. If you honor them through life by letting them know that their sacrifices were not in vain. They will share with you their ideas and wisdom on how to acquire your own freedom.

Remember, there are numerous Papa and Uncle aakhu from various nations because North America was a dumping ground for Africans from different countries in Africa. You may have a Papa Kongo (Kongo descendant) or Uncle Ga (GaDangme descendant). Follow your intuition and trust that if you are honest, your aakhu will identify themselves to you. Here's a simple prayer for Papa and Uncle Aakhu:

Papa fill in the blank and/or Uncle fill in the blank, thank you for your sacrifice. Thank you being a strong support and a pillar in my life. Know that your sacrifice was not in vain and I ask that you share your wisdom and fighting spirit to help me in my plight.

Prayer for Momma (Big Momma) and Auntie Aakhu
Similar to Papa and Uncle Aakhu, these were the first young African women to be kidnapped and brought to North America. These women were abducted from various tribes so it is possible to have a Momma Kongo, Momma Ebo, or Auntie Fon, and so on. It is believed that many of these women have fond memories

of Africa as well and were familiar with the healing arts and herbal remedies. Like the Papa and Uncle aakhu, they long for freedom and the escape from numerous abuses, particularly sexual abuse, so they created various remedies to protect themselves, their men, their children and eventually the whole community.

They like Papas and Uncles were cherished and respected in the slave community because of the wisdom they brought from Africa, their herbal knowledge and divination skills. Again, it is racist propaganda to believe that these women were solely concerned about the slave master and his family, as portrayed in many slave films. The Spirit of Mommas and Aunties of the past is the same Spirit in the Big Mommas and Aunties of today babysitting our children, passing down folk knowledge from times past, using herbal remedies to cure colds, earaches, and flus; and, if you allow her, she will divine for you using the bible or some other tool. Out of respect, many people call their Momma and Auntie aakhu La Madama, but you can call her whatever she prefers.

Again, like Papa and Uncle aakhu, Momma and Auntie spirits are also very entrepreneurial. This energy is seen in the life of the infamous Marie Leveau who belongs to this same class of spirits. They are strong, proud and bold feminine spirits.

When Momma and Auntie aakhu feel that their sacrifices were in vain, they will clam up and not share anything with you. They will see you heading for your downfall or about to have an accident, and they will not step in to save you but allow it to happen. When they are appreciated, they share wisdom hidden in stories and guide you away from danger.

Momma <u>fill in the blank</u> and/or Auntie <u>fill in the blank</u>, thank you for your sacrifice, guidance and herbal wisdom. Help me to make life easier.

Let's restore the memory of these brave souls to a state of glory.

Prayer for Black Hawk Native American Spirits

Everyone has their own idea and image of Black Hawk but for me, I am reminded of the relationship between the escaped enslaved Africans and some Native Americans who hid them particularly in Florida and Louisiana. For me, when I think of Black Hawk, I always see an elderly Native American man sitting or standing at the edge of some rough terrain. When slave catchers, bounty hunters and passerby's encounter him, they assume that he is just a displaced and superstitious old man. When they ask if he has seen runaways or other escapees, he usually directs them in an opposite direction or does not tell them anything at all. Once the coast is clear, the runaways hiding just a few feet away in the brush, the forests, the swamps, etc. thank the indigenous elder and either continue their voyage up North or into terrain that the slave catchers will not pursue.

So, in my mind's eye, Black Hawk does not just refer to the Sauk leader but honors the Folsom people, the indigenous Paleo-Indian culture that occupied most of North America, and the other Native Americans who misdirected spiritual and physical foes. They sit or stand at the edge of borders; hence Black Hawk is being on the wall. Black Hawk's name also conjures up image of an actual black hawk, thus being a spirit he can call upon this particular animal, which has keen eyesight. This animal gives him mystical sight that allows him to see potential dangers beforehand. Black Hawks I believe fight for justice and offer protection to those being denied basic liberties and rights. Hence my simple prayer to Black Hawk is:

Thank you for standing and being a protection on the wall.

Prayer for Sweet Water Native American Spirits

As escaped enslaved Africans flee from their kidnappers, I imagine that occasionally they came in contact with many Native American tribes. Many of the Native Americans were sympathetic to their cause. Some of the Native American women knowing the consequences for aiding and abetting runaway slaves and interfering in the white man's affairs. Ignored the laws and assist the runaways any way they can by hiding them when possible, and providing them with food, as they make their haste to freedom. Through these interactions, cultural exchange occurs and the Africans learn about Native American pharmacology and foodstuffs. These brave and strong Native American feminine spirits I believe are still present and responsible for dishes like cornbread, corn mush (cereal), succotash, etc.

Sweet Waters can still be seen in Native American women who are proud of their heritage and will not hesitate to call out an injustice done to their people or any people. Her generous and rebellious spirit influence others to assist us even if they are not fond of us because of our ethnic and/or cultural differences.

Thank you, Sweet Waters, for your compassion and generosity. Continue to fight and resist on my behalf so that we all can prosper.

Simple Invocations for the Netcharu

Here are some simple evocations that can be said to honor the netcharu. I have found that by saying simple affirmative evocations, the spirits of the netcharu will give you insight and suggestions on how to achieve that objective. However, be mindful that when you ask your spirits for something that you must do your part. For instance, if you ask Osar for peace in your home, be prepared to do what you must to maintain peace in your home. There is no amount of peace incense, white flowers, etc. that is going to substitute the work you need to do. Know that these are tools and they will help but you have to do your part as if you never asked for help in the first place.

Thank you Npus for opening the way for better opportunities, food good health and good luck, for me and those whom I love. Thank you for closing the way to that which would do me and those whom I love harm.

Thank you Osar for peace, prosperity and knowledge.
Thank you Djahuti for wisdom and repairing my eye to avoid the trappings of Set.
Thank you Hru for success and giving me victory over my enemies.
Thank you Hru Aakhuti for protecting me from danger seen and unseen.
Thank you Oset for fulfillment and providing for all of my needs.
Thank you Nebhet for helping me to get whatever I want.
Thank you, Maat, for wealth, prosperity, balance and order.
Thank you, Sokar, for perfect health.

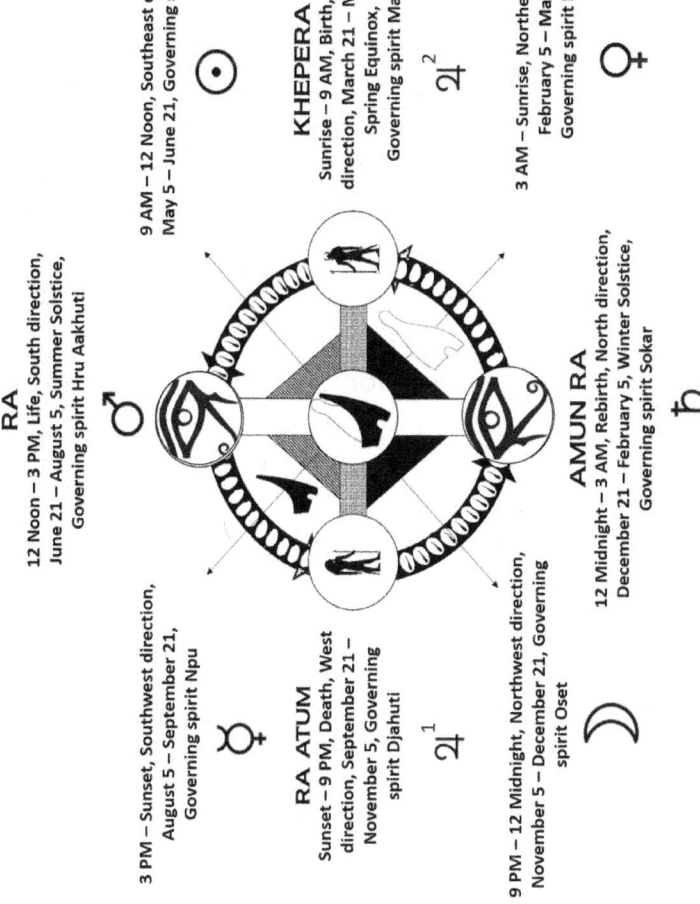

RA
12 Noon – 3 PM, Life, South direction, June 21 – August 5, Summer Solstice, Governing spirit Hru Aakhuti

KHEPERA
Sunrise – 9 AM, Birth, East direction, March 21 – May 5, Spring Equinox, Governing spirit Maat

9 AM – 12 Noon, Southeast direction, May 5 – June 21, Governing spirit Hru

3 AM – Sunrise, Northeast direction, February 5 – March 21, Governing spirit Nebhet

3 PM – Sunset, Southwest direction, August 5 – September 21, Governing spirit Npu

RA ATUM
Sunset – 9 PM, Death, West direction, September 21 – November 5, Governing spirit Djahuti

9 PM – 12 Midnight, Northwest direction, November 5 – December 21, Governing spirit Oset

AMUN RA
12 Midnight – 3 AM, Rebirth, North direction, December 21 – February 5, Winter Solstice, Governing spirit Sokar

Guardian Spirit & Number	Planet	Time of the Day	Time of the Year
Amun Ra Moment			
Sokar, 13 & 17	Saturn ♄	12 AM to 3 AM	Dec. 21–Feb. 5
Nebhet, 5	Venus ♀	3 AM to Sunrise	Feb. 5–Mar. 21
Khepera Moment			
Maat, 2 & 4	Jupiter ♃²	Sunrise to 9 AM	Mar. 21–May 5
Hru, 6	Sun ☉	9 AM to 12 PM	May 5–June 21
Ra Moment			
Hru Aakhuti, 3, 4, 7 and 11	Mars ♂	12 PM to 3 PM	June 21–Aug. 5
Npu, 3, 9, 21	Mercury ☿	3 PM to Sunset	Aug. 5–Sep. 21
Ra Atum Moment			
Djahuti, 8	Jupiter ♃¹	Sunset to 9 PM	Sep. 21–Nov. 5
Oset, 7	Moon ☽	9 PM to 12 AM	Nov. 5–Dec. 21

Select Bibliography

Amen, Ra Un Nefer. *Metu Neter Vol. 1: The Great Oracle of Tehuti and the Egyptian System of Spiritual Cultivation.* Khamit Media Trans Visions Inc, 1990

Browder, Anthony T. *From the Browder File: 22 Essays on the African American Experience.* Institute of Karmic Guidance, 1989.

Browder, Anthony T. *Nile Valley Contributions to Civilization.* Institute of Karmic Guidance, 1992.

Budge, E.A. Wallis. *An Egyptian Hieroglyphic Dictionary Vol. I and II.* New York: Dover Publication, 1978.

Budge, E.A. Wallis. *Osiris & The Egyptian Resurrection, vols. 1 & 2.* Dover Publications, 1973.

Chadwick, David and Suzuki, Shunryu *To Shine One Corner of the World: Moments with Shunryu Suzuki.* Broadway; 2001.

Eker, T. Harv. *Secrets of the Millionaire Mind: Mastering the Inner Game of Wealth.* HarperBusiness, 2005.

Fu-Kiau, K. Kia Bunseki. *African Cosmology of the Bantu-Kongo: Principles of Life & Living.* Athelia Henrietta Press, 2001.

Harner, Michael. *The Way of the Shaman.* Harper One; 10 Anv. edition, 1980

Hollenweger, W. J. *The Pentecostals: The Charismatic Movement in the Churches.* Augsburg Publishing House, 1972.

Huson, Paul. *Mastering Witchcraft: A Practical Guide for Witches, Warlocks and Covens*. Perigee Trade, 1980.

Kaslow, Andrew J. and Claude F. Jacobs. *The Spiritual Churches Of New Orleans: Origins, Beliefs, And Rituals Of An African American*. University of Tennessee Press, 2001.

Kurzweil, R. 2012. *How To Create A Mind: The Secret of Human Thought Revealed.* New York: Penguin Group.

MacGaffey, Wyatt. *Custom and Government in the Lower Congo*. University of California Press, 1970.

MacGaffey, Wyatt. *Religion and Society in Central Africa: The BaKongo of Lower Zaire.* The University of Chicago Press, 1986.

Miranda and Stephen Aldhouse-Green. *The Quest for the Shaman: Shape-Shifters, Sorcerers and Spirit Healers in Ancient Europe.* Thames and Hudson, 2005.

Moore, Derric. *Kamta: A Practical Kemetic Path for Obtaining Power*. Four Sons Publications, 2011

Moore, Derric. *Maa: A Guide to the Kemetic Way for Personal Transformation*. Four Sons Publications, 2012

Moore, Derric. *Maa Aankh: MAA AANKH: Finding God the Afro-American Spiritual Way, by Honoring the Ancestors and Guardian Spirits.* Four Sons Publications, 2010

Moore, Derric. *Maa Aankh: MAA AANKH:* Discovering the Power of I AM Using the Shamanic Principles of Ancient Egypt for Self-Empowerment and Personal Development. Four Sons Publication, 2013

Synan, Vinson. *The Holiness-Pentecostal Movement in the United States.* William B. Eerdmans Publishing Company, 1971.

Thompson, Robert Farris. *Flash of the Spirit: African and Afro-American Art and Philosophy.* Random House, 1983.

Thompson, Robert Farris. *Face of the Gods: Art and Altars of Africa and the African Americas.* Prestel, 1993.

Thornton, John. *Africa and Africans in the Making of the Atlantic World, 1400-1800.* Cambridge University Press; 2 ed., 1998

INDEX

Aakhu, 24, 69, 70, 81, 82, 83, 84, 86, 93, 99, 104, 106, 109
Aapepu, 24, 73, 85
Ab, 19
affirmations do not work, 37
African cosmology, 6
Amun Ra, 49, 52, 56, 57, 58, 60, 64, 103, 158, 159, 160, 161, 162, 165, 166, 173, 179, 194, 195, 196, 198, 199, 213
Amun Ra (the Hidden Name of Ra, 158
Amun Ra Moment, 60, 213
Amun Ra rests, 160
ancestral spirits. *See* Aakhu & Aapepu
Auntie spirits. *See* La Madama

BA, 19
Bantu-Kongo philosophy, x, 6
born again, 59

constructive magick, 145
Council of Nicea, 182
Creolized Kongo cosmogram, 47

destructive magick, 146
Djahuti, 23, 60, 85, 129, 131, 176, 177, 178, 213
El Congo, 86

emergency magick, 187

fasting, 36, 37, 40, 116, 143, 158, 160
foe spirits, 68, 71
Folsom, 132, 209
fulfillment, Oset, 172

gestures. *See* special movements
Glyphs or sigils, 38
good versus evil, 8
good versus spiritual power, *22*
guardian spirits, iv, xi, 19, 22, 58, 68, 82, 102, 103, 119, 120, 121, 123, 162, 190

Holiness, 216
holistic living, 27
Hru, 23, 54, 59, 60, 68, 74, 79, 83, 84, 85, 86, 101, 110, 120, 130, 131, 132, 133, 134, 135, 138, 140, 155, 172, 174, 175, 176, 177, 178, 180, 181, 182, 184, 185, 203, 213
Hru Aakhuti, 23, 60, 84, 85, 86, 120, 130, 131, 132, 140, 184, 185, 203, 213

KAMTA (all caps), 6

Kemetic spirituality, 6, 45, 46, 48, 58
Khepera Moment, 60, 213
Kongo Cross, 46
Kushites (Ancient Nubians), 6

La Madama, 86, 87, 89
Lisa and Mawu. *See* Shu and Tefnut

maa khru, 178
Maat, 23, 37, 60, 83, 85, 86, 131, 132, 139, 203, 213
magick, xii, 4, 5, 14, 145, 187

Nebertcher, 62, 67, 68, 149, 186
Nebhet, 3, 23, 25, 60, 64, 84, 85, 101, 134, 141, 142, 143, 144, 175, 213
Npu, 23, 43, 58, 60, 64, 79, 82, 84, 125, 126, 127, 132, 133, 138, 141, 143, 174, 175, 201, 202, 203, 213

offering, 69, 111, 114, 115, 116, 123, 139, 142, 143, 144, 185, 203
offerings, 36
Old Kongo, 12, 118
Ole' Dirty Bastard, 91
Osar, 23, 24, 59, 68, 69, 70, 74, 75, 76, 81, 82, 85, 90, 100, 101, 103, 104, 110, 121, 123, 124, 125, 126, 128, 129, 133, 135, 141, 171, 172, 173, 174, 175, 176, 177, 178, 179, 180, 181, 182, 184, 188, 200
Oset, 23, 24, 48, 49, 60, 68, 83, 85, 101, 135, 150, 151, 153, 154, 155, 159, 165, 166, 167, 172, 173, 174, 175, 176, 177, 180, 203, 213

purpose of Story of Ra and Oset, 155

ra (personal power), 196
ra (personal spiritual power, 20
Ra Atum Moment, 60, 213
Ra Moment, 60, 213
Rau, ii, x, 20, 21, 22, 39, 125
ritual, ix, xi, xii, 4, 13, 14, 34, 35, 41, 77, 109, 144, 184, 185, 186, 188, 202

sacrifice, 36, 116, 142, 143, 144
sahu, 19, 21, 37, 38, 39, 41, 42, 69, 71, 73, 74, 80, 102, 166, 169, 170, 172, 184
salvation, 100, 160, 184, 191, 192, 194
self-conscious or spiritual heart. *See* Ab

Set, 24, 59, 68, 70, 73, 74, 75, 79, 85, 96, 100, 103, 110, 113, 123, 124, 125, 126, 128, 133, 170, 172, 173, 174, 175, 176, 177, 178, 179, 180, 181, 182
shamanism, ix, x, xi, 6, 11, 13, 22, 35
shemsu, 123
Shu and Tefnut, 9, 104, 150, 151
Sokar, 23, 60, 84, 85, 130, 138, 213
Soul. *See* Ab
special movements, 33, 35
spiritual bank, 193
Spiritual Light & Lesser Light (Darkness), 21
subconscious. *See* sahu
Superconscious. *See* BA

the 9:1 ratio, 124
The Science of Spiritual Light & Lesser Light (Darkness), 125
triage magick, 187
true of voice, 59

Yang and Yin. *See* Shu and Tefnut
Yoruba, 58, 115, 135

Author's Note

Thank you for allowing me to share my experience, story, and methods that I have found that worked for me with you. I hope that it empowered and improved your life the way it has touched mine.

If you enjoyed the book and have a minute to spare, I would really appreciate an honest review on the page or site where you purchase the book. Your review is greatly appreciated because reviews from readers like you, make a huge difference in helping new readers find practical spiritual books like this one.

Amazon Review: https://amzn.to/2LU30O8

1 SoL Alliance.com: http://bit.ly/2LU4iIY

Thank you!

Derric "Rau Khu" Moore

Other Books by the Author:

MAA AANKH Volume I:
Finding God the Afro-American Spiritual Way,
by Honoring the Ancestors and Guardian Spirits

Kamta: A Practical Kemetic Path for Obtaining Power

Maa: A Guide to the Kemetic Way for Personal Transformation

MAA AANKH Volume II:
Discovering the Power of I AM Using the Shamanic Principles of Ancient Egypt for Self-Empowerment and Personal Development

MAA AANKH Volume III:
The Kemetic Shaman Way of Working the Superconscious Mind to Improve Memory, Solve Problems Intuitively and Spiritually Grow Through the Power of the Spirits (Volume 3)

Honoring the Ancestors the Kemetic Shaman Way:
A Practical Manual for Venerating and Working with the Ancestors from a God Perspective

The Kamta Primer: A Practical Shamanic Guide for Using Kemetic Ritual, Magick and Spirituality for Acquiring Power

En Español: Maa Aankh Volume I:
Encontrando a Dios al Modo Espiritual Afroamericano, Honrando a los Ancestros y a los Espiritus Guardianes

Neter (God) Got Your Back!

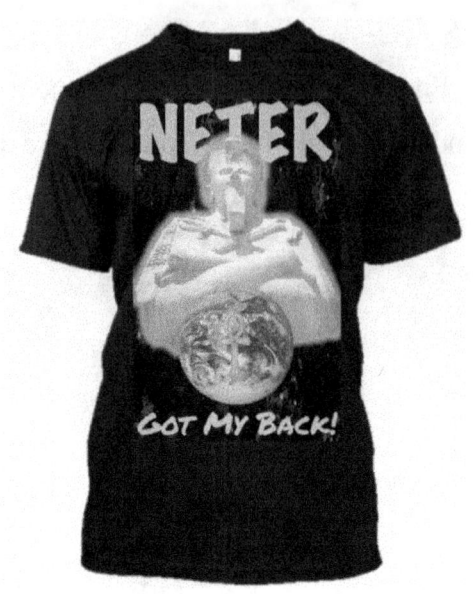

Purchase your empowering, enlightening and uplifting MKBN tees, hoodies and caps today at 1SoLAlliance.com

For more books on religion, astrology, numerology, chakras, prayer, reiki, self-help and metaphysical supplies, visit us at:

www.thelandofkam.com

www.1solalliance.com

www.ingramcontent.com/pod-product-compliance
Lightning Source LLC
Chambersburg PA
CBHW070941230426
43666CB00011B/2521